To Drink and To Eat

Treats & Tribulations from a French Kitchen

SELF PORTRAIT

in food!

If I were a fruit,
I'd be a melon:

Because a little girl
once thought my name
was Gui-Melon.

If I were a vegetable,
I'd be a tomato:

Because, with a drizzle
of olive oil and some
basil, it's simple
gastronomy.

If I were a type of
meat, I'd be a grilled,
bone-in prime rib:

No comment necessary.

If I weren't a fruit
or a vegetable,
I would be a cep:

If I were a fish,
I'd be whatever,
I guess:

I just love fish.

In a carpaccio with
some olive oil and
some foie gras.

If I were a cooking utensil,
I would be a knife:

Because, with a knife,
you can already cook
a lot of things.

If I were a comfort food,
I would be
spaghetti with garlic:

A dish so easy to
make that it is subject to
numerous debates
in Italy.

If I were a drink,
I would be coffee:

Because I drink it all
the time when I work.

If I were evil incarnate,
I would be a can of peas:

Because fresh peas
are so good.

If I were a dessert,
I'd be a chocolate
lava cake:

But I don't have a
big sweet tooth.

If I were an ingredient,
I'd be milk:

Because I'm amazed by
everything that you can
make with just milk.

lon.

To Drink and To Eat

Treats & Tribulations from a French Kitchen

— GUILLAUME LONG —

Volume 3

Colors by Céline Badarous Denizon
and Guillaume Long

AN ONI PRESS PUBLICATION

This book is dedicated to everyone who has waited for it.

G. L.

English Translation by Sylvia M. Grove
Lettering by AndWorld Design's Fernando Fuentes
Colors by Céline Badarous Denizon and Guillaume Long
Cover Art by Guillaume Long
Front Cover Design by Robin Allen & Angie Knowles
Cover Jacket Design by Kate Z. Stone
Interior Design by Angie Knowles & Kate Z. Stone
Editing and Localization by Amanda Meadows

The "Pépé Roni" comic strips are the work of artist Mathias Martin and originally appeared in the magazine *French Cuisine*.
Pages 18-19 were originally created for the magazine *Pop Corn*.
Pages 65-69 and pages 98-99 were originally created with a different text and a different order for the online project Web Trip
(http://www.webtrip-comics.com/fr/), an initiative of the Lyon BD Festival.

Published by Oni-Lion Forge Publishing Group, LLC.

James Lucas Jones, president & publisher • Charlie Chu, e.v.p. of creative & business development • Steve Ellis, s.v.p. of games & operations
Alex Segura, s.v.p of marketing & sales • Michelle Nguyen, associate publisher • Brad Rooks, director of operations • Amber O'Neill, special
projects manager • Margot Wood, director of marketing & sales • Katie Sainz, marketing manager • Henry Barajas, sales manager
Tara Lehmann, publicist • Holly Aitchison, consumer marketing manager • Troy Look, director of design & production • Angie Knowles,
production manager • Kate Z. Stone, senior graphic designer • Carey Hall, graphic designer • Sarah Rockwell, graphic designer • Hilary
Thompson, graphic designer • Vincent Kukua, digital prepress technician • Chris Cerasi, managing editor • Jasmine Amiri, senior editor
Shawna Gore, senior editor • Amanda Meadows, senior editor • Robert Meyers, senior editor, licensing • Desiree Rodriguez, editor • Grace
Scheipeter, editor • Zack Soto, editor • Ben Eisner, game developer • Jung Lee, logistics coordinator • Kuian Kellum, warehouse assistant

Joe Nozemack, publisher emeritus

1319 SE Martin Luther King Jr. Blvd.
Suite 240
Portland, OR 97214

onipress.com ● ● ● lionforge.com

lemonde.fr/blog/long
facebook.com/0c0ABAM
twitter.com/0c0ABAM
instagram.com/0c0ABAM

First Edition: February 2022

ISBN: 978-1-63715-014-6
eISBN: 978-1-63715-023-8

1 2 3 4 5 6 7 8 9 10

Library of Congress Control Number 2021941331

Printed in China.

Contents

Manual

 Level 1: Recipes requiring no previous culinary knowledge. Quick, with no actual cooking involved.

 Level 2: Recipes that are slightly more involved, take some time, and require some amount of cooking.

 Level 3: Very difficult recipes (only sometimes; I'm mostly joking).

 Ego Trip: Stories that feature my mug(shot).

 Restaurant: Stories of meals in places that I like.

 Inventory: Useful lists for foodies.

 Joël Reblochon: Cooking tips and history presented by the late Joël Reblochon.

 Mr. Publisher: Spontaneous interjections from Oni-Lion Forge executives in order to improve this book's readability, meaning its sales.

 Leftovers: Everything else that doesn't fit into the other categories of this book.

Spring

A Laugh at the Fish Market

I'm already cracking up, heheh hehheheh!

TODAY, YOU'RE AT YOUR LOCAL FISH MARKET, YOUR LIST IN HAND...*

FIVE LITTLE FISHIES SWIMMIN' IN THE SEA

SALMON, RED MULLET, SWORDFISH, MONKFISH, SARDINES-- THE CHOICE IS YOURS.

BUT WAIT. TODAY, YOU WANT TO JOKE AROUND A LITTLE FIRST.

So... I'll take your stingray.

(Heh well not that way.)

It looks rather tasty.

kr kr

Heh, you know-hatim-sayin.

AND THAT'S NORMAL.

A STINGRAY IS A FISH THAT PERMITS AN EXPLORATION OF THE FASCINATING WORLD OF INNUENDO.

Is your stinger pretty fresh?

I imagine that you have your pick of the date.

mh.

mh.

Heh heh!

Huh 'kay sorry

BUT HERE, YOU GO DEEPER.

Is your stinger cleaned?

You sure? Yep.

Yep.

And it didn't hurt?

'Scuse me?

Heh heh nothing.

Listen, are you buying any or Yes

yes I'll take the stinger hehe...

EXCEPT, HERE YOU ARE... ALL GOOD JOKES COME TO AN END, AND ONCE YOU'RE HOME WITH YOUR STINGRAY (OR SKATE), HOW SHOULD WE SAY IT:

Oh, Shiiiiit...

What the heck do I do with this thing?

I don't think I'm even supposed to flour it.

And it cost me an arm and a leg!

IT'S NO FUN.

COME ON, GET A GRIP. TODAY, YOU'RE GOING TO COOK A...

SKATE WITH BLACK BUTTER SAUCE

But I don't know how to cook!

Anyway, didn't they stop selling skate with black butter sauce from restaurants because it gives you cancer?

Right?

*SEE TDTE VOLUME 1

YES... OR MAYBE IT GOT BANNED BECAUSE OF YOUR KINDS OF JOKES...

The chef's stinger is perfect!

AS YOU CAN SEE.

AT ANY RATE, TO MAKE THIS DISH, YOU NEED THE FOLLOWING INGREDIENTS:

(FOR TWO PEOPLE)

AN ONION

A CARROT

BAY LEAVES

TWO SKATE WINGS, PEELED AND NOT TOO FATTY

A LEMON

RED WINE VINEGAR

SALT

PEPPER

ITALIAN PARSLEY

BUTTER

CAPERS IN VINEGAR

1. BEGIN BY PEELING THE CARROT AND ONION AND CUTTING THEM UP HOWEVER:

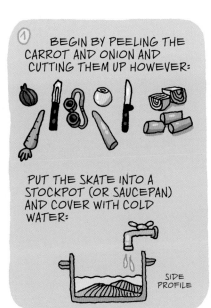

PUT THE SKATE INTO A STOCKPOT (OR SAUCEPAN) AND COVER WITH COLD WATER:

SIDE PROFILE

2. ADD THE CUT CARROTS AND ONIONS, A BAY LEAF, AND SOME SALT AND PEPPER:

AND ACTUALLY, YOU'RE IN THE PROCESS OF MAKING A COURT BOUILLON, A LIQUID FOR POACHING SEAFOOD. IT'S LIKE UNDERWEAR, IN THAT IT'S VERY PERSONAL. YOU COULD ADD SOME GARLIC, SAGE, THYME... WHATEVER YOU WANT. YOU CAN EVEN STICK THE ONION WITH SOME CLOVES:

3. NEXT ADD ONE

Umm... Wait I didn't catch something... I have to put my underwear on the stinger?

(huhuh) NO.

Well okay then, huhuh!

IT WAS A METAPHOR.

3. SO, NEXT ADD ONE OR TWO TABLESPOONS OF VINEGAR INTO THE WATER AND BRING IT TO A BOIL:

flopflopflop

LOWER THE HEAT AND LET IT SIMMER, UNCOVERED, FOR AROUND TEN MINUTES:

4. WHILE THAT GENTLY FLOPFLOPS, MAKE THE BLACK BUTTER SAUCE THAT THE RECIPE IS NAMED FOR:

MELT A GOOD BIT OF BUTTER (LIKE, ALMOST A STICK) IN A PAN:

FSHHHH

AND HERE'S WHERE YOU'LL GET CANCER (AFTER THE 125,978TH TIME THAT YOU MAKE THIS RECIPE) WELL ANYWAY, CALMLY LET THE BUTTER DEEPLY DARKEN:

KRSHKR

OR, YOU COULD JUST LET THE BUTTER BROWN, AND THAT'S JUST AS GOOD:

SHHHH

DEGLAZE THE PAN WITH A DASH OF VINEGAR OR A LITTLE BIT OF LEMON JUICE:

RFRSHHHH

5. ADD SOME DRAINED CAPERS AND CHOPPED PARSLEY INTO THE PAN (WHATEVER QUANTITY YOU WANT):

AND REMOVE FROM THE HEAT. SEASON WITH SALT & PEPPER:

6. FINALLY, REMOVE THE SKATE FROM THE COURT BOUILLON WITH A SLOTTED SPOON, AND POUR YOUR ~~BLACK~~ BROWN BUTTER SAUCE OVER ALL.

Here you go!

♪ My stinger is drained and ready for sauce! ♪

Haha, I'm kidding.

IF THERE'S STILL SOME SKIN ON YOUR RAY, GO AHEAD AND REMOVE IT.

Yeah, itsh not bad.

Itsh tough though!

Hey, next time I'm going to ask the butcher about his sausage.

And ask the milk-man if his wife has nice jugs!

Huh huh!

DON'T TALK WITH YOUR MOUTH FULL. ENJOY!

leon.

What if you put a mascot in your recipes? Create reader loyalty, like Walt Disney did.

Something like Brayden?

Noo. More cute.

I'll try.

"Loveable."

Just do it or don't. There is no try.

Women are suckers for mascots.

Since cooking is for girls!

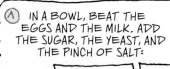

① IN A BOWL, BEAT THE EGGS AND THE MILK. ADD THE SUGAR, THE YEAST, AND THE PINCH OF SALT:

THEN SLOWLY ADD IN THE FLOUR.

Wha... What's this shit?

An otter?

A shitty otter.

B...but you said make it cute!

FYI, no one's given a damn about otters since 2006.

An otter.

Do this to me, the historic publisher of Jean-Paul Sartre! Shit, it's enough to give you nausea!

The secret to a successful muffin batter is to barely mix in the flour. Your goal is to make a lumpy batter that will make the muffin melt in your mouth. Don't follow the recipe, no matter what it says.

Nothing's set in stone, my friends!

Especially regarding muffins!

Nooka-ylook I'm getting really tired.

But I—

Really.

Sh.

And then... I dunno... make yourself a little more captivating! Put some eyes behind your glasses or something, like they recommend in "Marie Comic."

B...but...

You said that they weren't real journalists.

NO ONE GIVES A SHIT, DAMN IT!

We need them to sell our stuff... What now? Why are you looking at me like that?

Well, I, uh... I'm using my eyes.

Good. Carry on with the recipe, so that we can be done with it.

Ashtray.

② NEXT, ADD IN THE VERY SOFT BUTTER (OR SOME MELTED BUTTER THAT HAS BEEN COOLED) WITHOUT MIXING TOO CRAZILY. I MEAN IT:

THE RIGHT CONSISTENCY

THE WRONG CONSISTENCY

DIVIDE THE BATTER AMONG SOME CUTE AND COLORFUL SILICONE MUFFIN LINERS (THOSE THAT TEMPT YOU IN STORES EVERYWHERE).

(WITHOUT FILLING TO THE TOP)

"BAKE FOR 20 TO 30 MINUTES AT 400°F (ACCORDING TO HOW YOU LIKE THEM)."

That's it?

For the batter, yes.

You make muffins without anything in them?

Um no, no, I'm working on it.

③ TO GARNISH YOUR MUFFINS, HERE ARE SEVERAL BASIC IDEAS:

RASPBERRIES
(MY FAVORITE)

CHOCOLATE, BANANA, WALNUTS

PUMPKIN,
HAZELNUTS,
CINNAMON

SUN-DRIED TOMATOES,
OLIVES, MOZZARELLA

ZUCCHINI,
PANCETTA

APPLE, CINNAMON,
GINGER

STRAWBERRIES,
RICOTTA

BASIL,
LIME

BUTTERNUT SQUASH, BLUE CHEESE

PARMESAN,
SMOKED SALMON

FONTINA, WALNUTS

SWEET

LEMON CURD, POPPY SEEDS

MATCHA GREEN TEA
(IN POWDER OR
INFUSED INTO
THE MILK)

SAVORY

Mmm... bold. Incomplete, technically vague, but bold.

It's lacking something to bring it all together.

That said–

A bit of soul.

Aren't I loveable, now?

Meh.

With my eyes?

Milk is more loveable than you.

Oh.

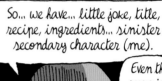

So... we have... little joke, title, recipe, ingredients... sinister secondary character (me).

Even the running joke with the ashtray.

About that ashtray...

Here.

Saw that coming.

Could we... I dunno... at least avoid the final clincher?

Okay. I'll stop here.

WORKERS, UNITE IT IS THE HAND THAT FEEDS YOU WHICH YOU MUST BITE!

Good... and above all...

WORKERS TOILING FOR BREAD, CAN'T GET FROM UNDER THE MAN

TOIL UNTIL YOUR SPIRIT IS DEAD

W- what's this?

Slrrrp

?

SHIT! WHAT'S THIS NONSENSE?

It's heh... some guys in the street who...

REVOLUTION, DEAR WORKERS. COME WITH THE FIGHTING UNION ORGANIZE! WORKERS, UNITE! IT IS THE HAND THAT FEEDS YOU WHICH YOU MUST BITE BITE BITE BITE!

You'd almost call them

heh RAGGAE-MUFFINS.

lon.

ON GROWN-UPS AND GOOD TASTE

HEH-HM.

Good evening, kids!

← DISSERTATION

FINISH YOUR SOUP.

EAT YOUR GREEN BEANS.

ONE MORE CARROT AND YOU'RE DONE!

WHAT ABOUT YOUR BROCCOLI?

COME ON!

YOU RECOGNIZE, OF COURSE, THESE WORDS... THIS SITUATION...

MEALTIME IS OFTEN THE SETTING OF A BAD PLAY IN WHICH PARENTS AND CHILDREN CONFRONT ONE ANOTHER, WITH A FINAL ACT THAT CONCLUDES EVERY OTHER TIME WITH:

To your room.

Let's analyze the tension with a diagram.

PARENT

MEAL

KID

no comprehension

TIRED BECAUSE OF WORK

WOULD LIKE TO RELAX

STILL HAS "THINGS TO DO"

MEAL PREPARED WITH LOVE (IN SPITE OF THE SPINACH)

NEITHER WANTING TO SPEND TOO MUCH TIME AT THE TABLE (FOR DIFFERENT REASONS.)

Shuuut uppp!

HASN'T FINISHED PLAYING

FULL OF ENERGY

THE ADULT IS GOING TO EMPLOY CERTAIN STRATEGIES HERE, THE FIRST BEING WELL KNOWN BY EVEN THE YOUNGEST AMONG YOU: THE **AIRPLANE** TACTIC.

And a spoonful for mommy vrooooooom...

THAT MAYBE WORKED WHEN YOU WERE THREE... BUT WHO, REALLY, CAN MISTAKE BROCCOLI PURÉE FOR A BOEING 747?

NEXT COMES THE TECHNIQUE OF DISGUISE.

Honey, it's not a vegetable, it's Mr. Eggplant!

With eyes!

FINALLY, LOSING STEAM, GROWN-UPS OFTEN RESORT TO THE TECHNIQUE OF:

I'M **WARNING** YOU, YOU ARE NOT LEAVING THE TABLE UNTIL EVERYTHING'S **FINISHED**.

We believed for a long time that all that fighting was because parents... you know... they're adults and blah blah blah...

But it's not at all the case.

The real explanation for all this can be found in BIOLOGY!

OHHH

OOOOHHHH

OHHH

AS KIDS, YOUR PALATES ARE DEVELOPED FOR ACIDITY AND SWEETNESS. THAT WORKS WELL, BECAUSE BASICALLY ANYTHING SWEET IN ITS NATURAL STATE IS EDIBLE.

RUNTZ!

(PRETTY PRACTICAL IN A CERTAIN ERA.)

IF THIS ELEMENTARY NOTION OF BIOLOGY HAS ESCAPED YOUR PARENTS...

ACIDITY

KID KRYPTONITE

TASTE-LESS

SWEET SAUCE

FAT

...IT SEEMS TO HAVE BEEN WELL UNDERSTOOD BY THE FAST-FOOD INDUSTRY!

ONLY WITH GROWING UP DOES THE PALATE EVOLVE TOWARD MORE COMPLEX TASTES, LIKE BITTERNESS....

I can't believe that I used to hate wine, sllrrp!

When it's actually way better than soda!

FOR THIS REASON, TURNIPS, COFFEE, AND STINKY CHEESE THRILL ADULTS... GROSS, RIGHT?

GIVEN THESE CIRCUMSTANCES... HOW CAN YOU FIND A MIDDLE GROUND WITH YOUR PARENTS REGARDING WHAT **"TASTES GOOD"**?

I promise you celery's good, look: I'll even eat it RAW!

MMMM! CRUNCH!

If we add to this that ① adults are always right, and that ② vegetables (especially the bitter ones) are actually good for you...

You kids are in a hard place... but thankfully, there are some dishes that everyone can agree on...

Let's look, for example, at this recipe for...

~~CHERRY~~ TOMATOES WITH SESAME ~~SEEDS~~

CLAP!

BRAVO! CLAP!

YEAH! CLAP! CLAP!

CLAP! CLAP! BRAVO!

To make it, you'll need:

CHERRY TOMATOES (VEGETABLES)

SESAME OR POPPY SEEDS (GRAINS)

TOOTHPICKS

WATER (WATER) + SUGAR (HEM) + LEMON (FRUIT) THAT KEEPS THE CARAMEL FROM HARDENING

CARAMEL PREPARED BY AN ADULT (THEIR PARTICIPATION WILL HELP THEM BUY IN)

A DASH OF BAD FAITH

Stick each tomato with a toothpick:

Dip half of each tomato into the warm caramel:

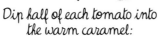

Finally, roll the tomatoes in the sesame or poppy seeds:

Add a dash of bad faith, and there you have your balanced meal of vegetables, grains, and fruit!

Don't hesitate to make very cute begging eyes... adults will get on board even faster!

And if you eat enough, maybe you will get out of eating your soup!

Until the next time!

lon.

LET'S COME BACK FOR A SECOND TO THIS RECIPE THAT SHOCKED ALL OF FRANCE... I'LL REMIND YOU OF THE CONTEXT: THE GOVERNMENT HAS JUST DECLARED A PERIOD OF AUSTERITY...

PURCHASING POWER HAS NEVER BEEN THIS LOW, WE ARE PREPARING FOR ENORMOUS BUDGETARY RESTRICTIONS, AND CREDIT RATING AGENCIES ARE THREATENING TO DOWNGRADE OUR TRIPLE A RATING...

AND YOU, YOU TURN UP WITH YOUR RECIPE!

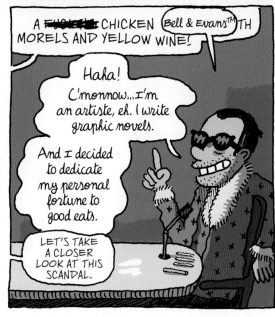

A ~~FUCKING~~ CHICKEN Bell & Evans™ TH MORELS AND YELLOW WINE!

Haha! C'monnow...I'm an artiste, eh. I write graphic novels.

And I decided to dedicate my personal fortune to good eats.

LET'S TAKE A CLOSER LOOK AT THIS SCANDAL.

CHICKEN

With morels and yellow wine

(From Bell & Evans™)

CORNSTARCH

YELLOW WINE

BELL & EVANS™ CHICKEN WITH GIBLETS

CRÈME FRAÎCHE

AN ONION

CLOVES

MORELS

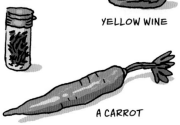

A CARROT

SHALLOTS

BUTTER

SAGE

THYME

BAY LEAVES

SALT

PEPPER

Obviously, that this dish costs a lot: yellow wine, morels, and a Bell & Evans™ chicken...

But c'monnow... a car, heh, that also costs a lot!

SIR, THE HONEST PEOPLE WHO READ YOUR COMICS DON'T GO TO WORK ON THE BACK OF A CHICKEN!

Haha!

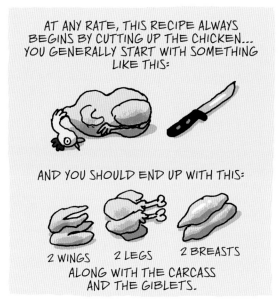

AT ANY RATE, THIS RECIPE ALWAYS BEGINS BY CUTTING UP THE CHICKEN... YOU GENERALLY START WITH SOMETHING LIKE THIS:

AND YOU SHOULD END UP WITH THIS:

2 WINGS   2 LEGS   2 BREASTS

ALONG WITH THE CARCASS AND THE GIBLETS.

WELL, SINCE IT CAN BE A LITTLE ~~SHITTY~~ TO CUT APART AND MAKE YOUR FINGERS GREASY AND GROSS, YOU CAN ALWAYS ASK YOUR BUTCHER TO DO IT:

That I cut up this chicken for you for a recipe with morels and yellow wine?

In the middle of a recession?

Jeepers, man.

I see how it is.

NEXT, YOU ARE GOING TO PREPARE THE STOCK, WITH:

THE CARROT, PEELED AND CUT IN HALF

THE ONION, PEELED AND STUCK WITH CLOVES

THE NECK, CARCASS, AND GIBLETS

BAY LEAVES, SAGE, AND THYME.

START IT OFF IN, SAY, ABOUT A QUART OF COLD WATER, AND LET IT COOK FOR AN HOUR OR SO ON LOW HEAT:

FLOP FLOP FLOP

THEN, LET THE STOCK COOL COMPLETELY, AND PLACE IT IN THE FRIDGE OVERNIGHT.

In this way, the stock will congeal. The fat will form a solid layer on the surface, and you can carefully skim it off with slotted spoon.

(This is a fat-skimming ladle)

SKIM THE FAT?

Yeah, like skimming off the top, heh heh!

HEY NO

Calm down, man.

SO... NEXT, YOU SHOULD THINK ABOUT SOAKING YOUR MORELS IN HOT WATER (OBVIOUSLY, THIS IS ONLY IF YOU BOUGHT THEM DRIED):

IN A LARGE POT OVER MEDIUM HEAT, LIGHTLY BROWN THE SHALLOTS AND THE CHICKEN PIECES IN BUTTER OR OIL:

PREPARE THE QUANTITY THAT YOU WANT, OF COURSE. USE THE EXTRA TIME TO MINCE SEVERAL SHALLOTS:

(YOU CAN CUT THE BREASTS IN HALF AND SEPARATE THE LEGS FROM THE THIGHS:)

STRAIN THE SKIMMED STOCK AND RESERVE THE GIBLETS:

ADD SOME CRÈME FRAÎCHE (I FIND 7 OZ TO BE ADEQUATE) AND THEN THE YELLOW WINE (ONE CUP). THEN COVER AND LET GENTLY SIMMER FOR ONE TO TWO HOURS:

THEN COVER THE CHICKEN PIECES WITH (SLIGHTLY WARMED) STOCK AND ADD THE GIBLETS (BECAUSE THEY'RE GOOD), THEN SEASON WITH SALT AND PEPPER, OF COURSE:

DO YOU AT LEAST HAVE ADVICE FOR THE YELLOW WI

It should be excellent.

My mom always told me that bad wine makes for a bad dish.

But I'm not going to name a producer, snirfl.

No one paid me enough to do itsnifl.

Oh, sorry

I BEG YOUR

Calm down.

Moving on.

BSO NEWSHOUR

WHEN THE CHICKEN IS COOKED, TRANSFER THE PIECES TO A HOT OVEN. COVER THEM WITH ALUMINUM FOIL SO THEY DON'T DRY OUT:

THEN ADD THE WELL-SCRUBBED (OR SOAKED) MORELS TO THE SAUCE, AND COOK, UNCOVERED, ON VERY LOW HEAT FOR AROUND TEN MINUTES:

THE SAUCE SHOULD REDUCE AND THICKEN A LITTLE. IF YOU NEED TO, MIX A LITTLE CORNSTARCH SEPARATELY INTO A CUP OF SAUCE, THEN STIR BACK INTO THE POT:

THERE YOU GO. YOU CAN ADD ANOTHER TOUCH OF YELLOW WINE TO THE SAUCE AND LET IT COOK FOR TWO MORE MINUTES.

Afterward, when you taste this chicken coated in yellow wine sauce perfumed with the scent of the morels and on a simple side of white rice, believe me, even if I made minimum wage, I would not hesitate to blow 6% of my paycheck on this dish.

I made minimum wage when I started out, BTW.

BUT, SIR! WHEN YOU THINK THAT IN FRANCE ALMOST TEN MILLION PEOPLE LIVE BELOW THE POVERTY LINE! YOU ARE UNETHICAL! DON'T YOU EVER THINK OF THEM?

Haha!

Bah, c'monnow, you could just as easily replace the yellow wine with table wine, the morels with white mushrooms, and the Bell & Evans chicken with Chicken McNuggets, but...

It's just less good.

Obviously.

Come on, what? I said something wrong?

Oh, calm down...

You're not going to lecture me about Marie Antoinette and her quip about the cake!

Get with the times, man!

YOUR COMPANY'S ANNUAL GET-TOGETHER. YOU'RE PLANTED NEXT TO THE BUFFET TABLE, A CUP OF PUNCH IN HAND, CONSIDERING A CASHEW NUT THAT IS JUST AS ALONE AS YOU ARE.

NOBODY SEEMS TO NOTICE EITHER OF YOU. WE MIGHT AS WELL SAY IT: NEITHER OF YOU ARE VERY INTERESTING. JUST TO BE HONEST.

THE ONLY THING A LITTLE FUN ABOUT YOU IS THE CHOREOGRAPHY OF "THE BOTTLE DANCE" THAT YOU LEARNED FOR YOUR STEPSISTER'S WEDDING.

BUT HERE, WITH ARCADE FIRE ON IN THE BACKGROUND, IT'S NO... HEY, ARE YOU LISTENING TO ME?

Huh?

Oh, I thought you were the narrator!

SORT OF, YES, BUT THAT IS NOT THE POINT.

Oooh, a voice inside me!

Like in "Innerspace"!

NOT AT ALL! FOR THE LOVE OF... OKAY. YOU'RE REALLY BANANAS, HUH.

Bananas? Hey now, I won't let you talk to me like that.

LISTEN... DO YOU WANT SOMEONE TO NOTICE YOU OR NOT?

Uh well... yeah, especially Valerie, who works in marketing, I um...

GOOD. LET'S GO SEE THIS VALERIE.

ACTUALLY, ABOUT BANANAS... ASK HER HOW THEY GROW.

W...what...just like that, straight up?

YES.

But she's talking now. I'm going to get myself kicked out!

DO WHAT I TELL YOU.

Several topics of discussion for WINNING at small talk

So whatdaya think, how do bananas grow?

I um

?

Is there a problem, Valerie?

Don't think so, no.

Well?

Er, how does a banana become a banana?

BINGO. YOU'VE CAUGHT HER ATTENTION.

LIKE NINE OUT OF TEN PEOPLE, WHAT VALERIE IS GOING TO SAY IS THAT BANANAS GROW ON TREES.

With a trunk that...um... a kind of palm tree, right?

Around ten feet high with some uh...

A TREE THAT'S SUPPOSEDLY A KIND OF PALM TREE.

BETWEEN TEN AND FIFTEEN FEET HIGH.

AND FROM ITS LEAVES HANG BANANAS, EITHER INDIVIDUALLY OR IN CLUMPS, DEPENDING ON THE PERSON.

But uh...that's not how bananas grow?

Because well,

That sounds right...

NOT AT ALL. A BANANA TREE IS NOT A TREE BUT A KIND OF...GRASS.

BETWEEN 22 TO 50 FEET, ITS "TRUNK" IS MADE UP OF LEAVES WOUND AROUND EACH OTHER.

EACH BANANA TREE GROWS ONE BUNCH (OF ABOUT TWO HUNDRED BANANAS) THEN DIES AFTER IT'S HARVESTED.

NEVERTHELESS, BANANA TREES EMIT UNDERGROUND OFFSHOOTS THAT MAKE OTHER BANANA TREES.

NOT SURPRISING THAT THE BANANA IS ONE OF THE MOST CONSUMED FRUITS IN THE WORLD!

VALERIE SHOULD ANSWER

Oh!

She's TALKING to me.

Duh! I'm an idiot, I have a banana tree at home.

Is he be No.

No prob, it's cool.

"COOL." YOU'VE EARNED ONE POINT.

MOVE ON TO... HEY, WHAT ABOUT THE CASHEW?!

Are you new?

No, I've worked here for 19 years!

Are you familiar with cashews?

Uhm...

ABSOLUTELY NOT! IN FACT UHM...I...OKAY, GOT IT. AT THE BEGINNING, IT'S A FRUIT OF THE ANARCH... ANORA... NO, ANACARDIACEAE FAMILY, WHICH IS A KIND OF TREE. ON THE BOTTOM OF THIS FRUIT GROWS A POD THAT CONTAINS THE NUT. WHEN THIS POD IS GRILLED, YOU CAN REMOVE THE SHELL, AND BAM!

A CASHEW!

Ooh b...but how do you know all that, Mr. uh—

Call me Christian

you ow him? No.

Let's just say I'm cultivated, no pun intended.

Haha

Who is this guy

And Brussels sprouts, eh?

BRUSSELS SPR... I KNOW NOTHING ABOUT THE...

Don't worry. My dad grew them.

Who are you talking to?

To Christian.

Haha!

He's so funny!

Hem. Let's see.

I would say like this?

AAAAAND NO. WHILE IT DEFINITELY STARTS AS A SPOUT, YOU ONLY HARVEST THE BUDS ON ITS FLOWERING STALK. YOU HARVEST AROUND FIFTY BUDS PER STALK AFTER ABOUT 100 DAYS.

Oooh!

THAT'S GREAT, CHRISTIAN!

YOU HAVE WON OVER YOUR AUDIENCE!

NOW, ONTO **SAFFRON**.

Sooo? Anyone?

I haven't the foggiest.

Saffr What d he sa

Get outta

C'mon Wikipedia this shit

Come on, it's easy.

Right?

THE FLOWER OF THE CROCUS SATIVUS, LADIES AND GENTLEMEN, OR RATHER, ITS STIGMA! HARVESTED AS SOON AS THE FLOWER BLOSSOMS AND BEFORE TEN O'CLOCK IN THE MORNING, YOU NEED AROUND 45,500 STIGMA IN ORDER TO OBTAIN ONE POUND!

Good lord!

And five pounds of fresh stigmas for one pound of saffron as we know it.

Hence the price.

Exactly.

Oh yeah?

How bout peanuts?

IT'S A LITTLE PLANT WITH YELLOW FLOWERS CALLED ARACHIS HYPOGAEA THAT PRODUCES ITS FRUIT UNDERGROUND AND THIS FRUIT...WELL...IS THE PEANUT.

GNMFF!

AH, HERE THEY ARE!

THEY COME FROM THE PEA FAMILY, HENCE THEIR NAME.

IN CONTRAST, THE ENDIVE DOESN'T GROW IN THE GROUND. INSTEAD, IT GROWS IN THE DARK (WHICH GIVES IT ITS WHITE COLOR BECAUSE CHLOROPHYLL CAN ONLY DEVELOP WITH SUNLIGHT). IT'S A ROOT THAT IS TRIMMED AND REGROWS A HEAD, AND THIS HEAD, IT'S...

IT'S?

AN ENDIVE?

WELL DONE.

HEH HEH. SPEAKING OF ENDIVES, TAKE A LOOK AT YOUR COLLEAGUES' FACES:

HOW DOES HE DO THAT?

OH YEAH. YOU FOR THE WIN.

SAY GOODBYE TO THE OLD YOU, VEGETATING BY THE BUFFET TABLE UNNOTICED BY THE WORLD. YOU'RE BECOMING THE ALPHA MALE.

valérie ♡

IT'S A COMFORTABLE PLACE, BUT IT'S DIFFICULT TO HOLD ONTO. YOUR JEALOUS COLLEAGUES WILL LOOK FOR ANY OPPORTUNITY TO TRY TO TEAR YOU DOWN.

?

What about broccoli?

That's right!

Hmm?

Oh yeah how does broccoli grow, showof

I... ehh... I... mh...

INSPIRATION.

I'M STILL HERE. DON'T PANIC.

In fact, few people know that it's actually a flower.

CONFIDENCE.

Oh

Specifically, the beginning of the flowering of a cabbage.

HUMILIATION.

Oh

Anything else?

Asparagus? Now I think that's heavy

SIMPLE.

Yeah!

Well pla

CLAP CLAP

FACE OF A BETA MALE

Ah... you plant a collection of roots (called a "CROWN"), and "SHOOTS" emerge from this three years later. And these shoots, well... those are the asparagus.

CRKK

STALK

GROUND

ROOTS

WHEN THEY ARE GREEN, THEY HAVE BEEN EXPOSED TO LIGHT DURING THEIR GROWTH. WHEN THEY ARE WHITE, THEY'VE BEEN COVERED WITH SOIL.

And purple, hmm?

OOH

WOO

PURPLE, ONLY THE HEAD HAS BEEN EXPOSED TO LIGHT. A LITTLE LIKE YOURS

Ha ha

HAHAHA!

And...pineapple?

VALERIE IS BACK.

Not from a palm tree! Hehe!

GO FOR THE GOLD.

It's a herbaceous plant that grows on the ground. The pineapple grows from the end of a stem. You can easily grow them yourself from a pineapple crown!

So, you're good with pineapples... what about peaches?

Uhh...?

Women, c'mon!

Ehh ...

GO IN FOR THE KILL!

CHRISTIAN?

What are you looking at up there?

I...

AGH! OH NO!

Huh?

Well, women, I dunno

I KNOW A FEW THINGS ABOUT GARDENING, BUT FOR PICKING SOMEONE UP, YOU'RE ON YOUR OWN!

CLICK.

Women are great but not when you're in the weeds, heh heh...

Yeah okay.

WHAT AN IDIOT.

Nooo, don't leav

I'm getting another drink.

Wait, I'll come with you

No, thanks.

See you, Monday!

We'll see.

lon.

RMH...I...

GOOD EVENING.

THIS IS ELLIOT. FOR THE PURPOSE OF THIS STORY, HE TALKS AND HAS HANDS. IN REAL LIFE, HE'S CONTENT TO CHASE HIS TAIL AND SAY "WOOF."

AH, I SEE THAT YOU HAVE FOUND A MASCOT.

N...NO, MR. PUBLISHER, IT'S JUST... UHM...FOR THIS PARTICULAR STORY.

DOESN'T MATTER.

WE WILL SEE.

OH... OKAY.

CONTINUE.

IT IS SAID, HERE AND THERE, THAT HAUTE GASTRONOMY IS RESERVED FOR THE MOST FORTUNATE...

BIG MISTAKE.

TAKE A LOOK AT THIS:

THANK GOD I HAVE HANDS.

POORLY DRAWN NONETHELESS.

MOVING ON.

CONSIDER THIS...

Bone marrow

$1.50/LB!

A DOLLAR FIFTY PER POUND? I

UM--

WOOF WOOF!

AHEM EXCUSE ME. BACK TO IT.

YOU KNOW... BONE MARROW. THE THING THAT YOU ONLY REMEMBER IS GOOD AT THE END OF A STEW...

WHO WANTS THE MARROW?

ME

ME

ME ME

ME ME

ME ME

OKAY. WE'RE GOING TO SHARE.

NOBODY FOR THE LAST PIECE OF TURNIP?

WELL, GOOD NEWS, YOU DON'T HAVE TO WAIT FOR THE NEXT STEW OR OTHER OSSO BUCCO TO TASTE THIS DI-VINE FOOD!

FOLLOW ME INTO THE KITCHEN!

THESE HANDS ARE DEFINITELY PRACTICAL.

OVEN-GRILLED BONE MARROW

This guy, for example

Rub it with salt

Here

There

On a cookie sheet in the oven for a generous half-hour (450°F)

Voilà

SPREAD THE STILL-HOT MARROW ONTO A TOASTED PIECE OF BREAD

SKKSKR

HERE YOU GO. A LITTLE SEA SALT ON TOP...

NIRVANA ATTAINED.

COME AS YOU ARE, RIGHT?

OF COURSE, THIS RECIPE IS RESERVED FOR PURISTS, BECAUSE ALL THE FAT STAYS IN THE MARROW INSTEAD OF MELTING INTO A BROTH.

BUT IT'S SO GOOD...

LET'S MOVE ON TO THE OTHER RECIPE.

Being served: Being given a portion of a meal by another individual

Look at my library! L'Asso, Cornélius, Ego comme X, le Dernier Cri, Futuro...

I have all of them!

That's right, Guillaume. I love independent comics!

I even have Blanquet's book!

And all the editions of the fanzine "Fusée"!

This speaks to you, doesn't it?

MON MÉCHANT MOI

You KNOW VERY well that if I were President, the comic authors would be better treated.

But I Listened to. Respected. I

But I can't vote for you.

Why not, then? My parents are liberals...

I can't.

That's ridiculous!

Since when do you have to act like your parents? Give it a try!

EIGHT YEARS AFTER HAVING THIS STRANGE DREAM, I NOTE THAT I'M NOT GOOD AT PREDICTING THE FUTURE. I'M STILL A GRAPHIC NOVELIST, AND IT'S STILL NOT CONSIDERED A "SERIOUS" CAREER.

ON THE RIGHT AS WELL AS THE LEFT, THERE IS STILL LITTLE TO NO CONSIDERATION FOR A PROFESSION THAT CONCERNS ONLY A HANDFUL OF PEOPLE....

ooaaohah

THE INCREASE IN CONTRIBUTIONS TO FRANCE'S RETIREMENT SYSTEM (EFFECTIVE AS I AM WRITING THESE LINES) IS GOING TO COST ARTISTS A MONTH OF THEIR SALARY PER YEAR.

grmb

I can't stand genius books that I'm incapable of writing!

COMÉDIE SENTIMENTALE PORNOGRAPHIQUE BY JIMMY BEAULIEU

WE ARE NOT EVEN SALARIED. WE DON'T HAVE THE RIGHT TO UNEMPLOYMENT OR PAID VACATION. IT'S THE PRICE TO PAY FOR "DOING A JOB THAT YOU LOVE."

SHHHHHHHHHHHHH

CERTAIN COLLEAGUES THROW IN THE TOWEL. OTHERS FIND A "REAL JOB" ON THE SIDE TO SURVIVE. PARADOXICALLY, WE GENERATE A RATHER HEALTHY ECONOMIC OUTPUT...

I KNOW WELL THAT OUR NATIONAL PRIORITIES MUST (SHOULD) BE FULL-TIME WORK, INCREASED JOB SECURITY, AND STRENGTHENING THE EURO...

BUT ALL THE SAME, CULTURE (LIKE EDUCATION) REMAINS AN ACCESSIBLE MEDIUM THAT FIGHTS AGAINST SOCIAL INEQUALITIES AND OBSCURANTISM. MAYBE CULTURE MAKES US A LITTLE BETTER.

WHO CAN BE SATISFIED WITH A GOVERNMENT THAT SCORNS CULTURE?

lon.

★ COMPLÉMENTAIRE ET OBLIGATOIRE

I am aboard flight 1B3483 from Geneva to...

Madrid

(Relaxing music for dying to, the kind like in the movie "Soylent Green".)

I'm not stressed!

Everything's okay!

The guy who did the freefall from outer space must have been insane!

I'm headed there for a reading and book signing of *"A Comer y a beber,"* published by **SINS ENTIDO**.

Last night, I had dinner with my parents, who live just outside of Geneva. My mom always cooks a ton of food when I visit, and this time was no exception:

NO, UNDERSTAND, OVER THERE I DON'T KNOW IF YOU EVEN ARE GOING TO BE ABLE TO EAT. IT'S THEIR ECONOMY, YOU SEE. APPARENTLY, THE SPANIARDS DON'T EVEN HAVE ENOUGH MONEY TO GET A DIVORCE... SO, IF MY SON IS GOING THERE AS AN AMBASSADOR OF FRANCE, HE WILL NOT GO ON AN EMPTY STOMACH.

Staub® Dutch oven, for 8 people when filled to the brim

BUT MOOOOM...

ARE YOU FAMOUS IN SPAIN?

IF THAT'S THE CASE, YOU SHOULD SHAVE AND WEAR A DRESS SHIRT. THAT WOULD BE BETTER.

MOM!!!

Ⓐ A martini and tons of cashews (I admit she knows me well)

② Kidneys and mushrooms flambéed in Madeira wine, served over rice

③ Salmon-stuffed cabbage (a recipe created for former French President Mitterrand) for around 519,737 people

④ Cheese and frangipane, for dessert (served separately)

Actually, I think I should go home for a week and make a travel guide about my mom. I realize that on the airplane with the bresaola sandwich that she made me (a tradition from here on out). I won't be hungry for a week.

IN MY STOMACH.

Heyyy it's like Bourbon Street down here!

day 1

IT'S THE FOURTH TIME I'M GOING TO MADRID... THE GOOD PART OF HAVING NO SENSE OF DIRECTION IS THAT EACH TIME YOU VISIT A PLACE IS LIKE THE FIRST TIME.

(The night before)

January or not, I'm bringing summer clothes.

When in Madrid...

ALL OF THIS PROMISES TO BE AVERAGELY TERRIBLE. I DON'T EVEN KNOW IF I'M GOING TO HAVE ENOUGH MATERIAL FOR A JOURNAL.

CONCERNING MADRID'S GASTRONOMY, I ONLY REMEMBER THE FOLLOWING...

The MUSEO DEL JAMÓN isn't overly impressive, but the décor is really great because it's full of hanging hams.

CIEN MONTADITOS had not very good tapas with a mountain of chips in the middle.

One time, I tried a really expensive restaurant where I paid $40 for a veal chop with no sides.

AFTER I PASS THROUGH CUSTOMS, THERE IS A CROWD OF PEOPLE WAITING FOR ME WITH A BIG BANNER READING, "BIENVENIDO EN MADRID."

Holy shit, it's touching that all these people are glad that my plane didn't crash!

EN MADRID

ACTUALLY, NO, THEY AREN'T THERE FOR ME. INSTEAD, I FIND ROMAIN AND FANETTE FROM THE INSTITUT FRANÇAIS.

Hey, qué tal?

You can speak French if you want.

Haha que hables muy bien French...

Mh

WE ARE FRENCH.

Of course!

(Drawn from memory)

DURING MY STAY, I AM GOING TO SPEAK SPANISH (A LITTLE), ENGLISH (NOT BADLY, BUT NOT WELL), AND FRENCH. SOMETIMES ALL THREE IN THE SAME SENTENCE.

¿Y cuál es el tiempo en Madrid?

You... hah... you don't want to speak French?

¡No es mi pregunta!

'Ow ez ze weathair? (Is something wrong with this guy?)

Heyy wrong-o, hombre! Eye undairstayand el Español muy good!

Weather's been shitty.

Oh shit, no tengo a sweater!

Gracias, Fanette.

THE CAR THAT BRINGS ME TO THE HOTEL HAS **CD** MARKED ON THE LICENSE PLATE (MEANING DIPLOMATIC VEHICLE). I DON'T UNDERSTAND WHY WE DON'T BLOW MORE RED LIGHTS. MAYBE THERE ARE DRUGS IN THE TRUNK.

I rest for a bit in my suite on the Gran Vía. I should go explore a little, but since I already know Madrid so well...the Sagrada Família, the Park Güell, etc.

THIS SUCKS, THEY SHOULD HAVE GIVEN ME A ROOM WITH A VIEW OF THE OCEAN!

VIEW OF THE GRAN VÍA

SOFA AND BATHROOM 250 FEET THIS WAY

JUST THEN, I LOOK OUT THE WINDOW INTO THE STREET

Hey, that's crazy!

It looks like over there there's a...

NO......

YESSSSS?

YESSSSSS!!!

BURGER KING

HOME OF THE WHOPPER

A BURGAIR KEENG?!

BURGER KING. I HAD BEEN DENIED IN STOCKHOLM*, AND NOW I CAN FINALLY GET WHAT I'VE BEEN WAITING FOR. TO FINALLY EAT A WHOPPER AGAIN AFTER FIFTEEN YEARS.

Give me a "B"

Give me a "U"

THE BURGER KING DANCE

*SEE TDTE 2. YOU SHOULD HAVE ALREADY BOUGHT IT.

THIS TIME, I SOLEMNLY SWEAR TO NOT LEAVE MADRID WITHOUT HAVING GONE THERE. EVEN IF I HAVE TO DELAY MY FLIGHT HOME.

IN THE LOBBY, I MEET UP WITH SHEILA, WHO WORKS IN COMMUNICATIONS AT SINS ENTIDO, AND REGINA, WHO TRANSLATED THE FIRST VOLUME OF TDTE AND WHO WILL BE MY INTERPRETER FOR THE NEXT SEVERAL DAYS.

Hey, Sheila! "Give me your ha-and"

¡hola qué tal!

(What's he saying?)

(Dunno, sounds like a song.)

Oh.

SHEILA →

(Umm... doesn't he have a coat?)

REGINA

50°

(You know, Northerners are used to the cold*.)

*REGINA IS FROM MÁLAGA.

REGINA IS KIND OF THE EXTENSION OF MY VOICE. SO, IN THIS JOURNAL, I AM GOING TO DRAW HER AS IF SHE WERE A PUPPET:

NOTE: WHEN I WRITE IN PARENTHESES, THAT MEANS IT'S IN SPANISH (EXCEPT FOR THE SPEECH BUBBLE WHEN ROMAIN WAS CONFIDING IN FANETTE.) (AND EXCEPT WHEN USING THE NARRATIVE VOICE LIKE HERE. SINCE I DON'T SPEAK SPANISH, I'M NOT GOING TO THINK IN SPANISH. FOLLOW?)

Late afternoon, before my reading. I talk to several journalists. They systematically mistake me for a food critic (which actually would work well at restaurants).

The questions are interesting nonetheless. It feels like comics are taken very seriously here. More than in France, obviously.

THE READING AND THE BOOK SIGNING GOES WELL. ACTUALLY, THE ROOM IS PACKED.

¡PAREN AL MUNDO, QUE ME QUIERO BAJAR!

I EXPLAIN THAT I DON'T SPEAK SPANISH WELL BECAUSE MY HIGH SCHOOL TEACHER (MRS. FERRARI) GAVE US *MAFALDA* COMIC STRIPS TO ANALYZE. WHILE SHE WAS AN EXCELLENT TEACHER, I BECAME MORE INTERESTED IN QUINO'S DRAWINGS THAN IN SPANISH.

LA CENTRAL BOOKSTORE

EMOCIÓN

AFTERWARDS, WE'RE GOING TO HAVE SOME TAPAS. I HAVE COMPLETELY FOR-GOTTEN ABOUT THE NOTION OF "EATING". (I EVEN SKIPPED LUNCH...AND BY THAT, I MEAN, JUST A SANDWICH.) AT

LA CASA DEL ABUELO,

12 Calle de la Victoria, we have shrimp with garlic and olive oil with some wine (for me) and beer for the others:

bubbling oil

Spicy pepper

THE PLACE IS PACKED. THERE ARE A BUNCH OF FRAMES ON THE WALLS WITH OLD BLACK-AND-WHITE PHOTOS. THE TILES ARE COLORFUL, AND THERE ARE INSCRIPTIONS OF THE DISHES EVERYWHERE, FOR EXAMPLE "GAMBAS AL AJILLO," "GAMBAS A LA PLANCHA," "CROQUETAS DE GAMBA," "LANGOSTINOS PLANCHA," ETC.

THE TABLES ARE OPTIMAL FOR EATING SMALL PLATES WHILE STANDING:

(I DIDN'T BOTHER TO DRAW IT FULL OF PEOPLE, AS YOU CAN SEE.)

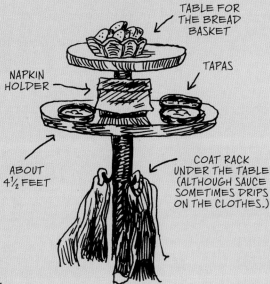

TABLE FOR THE BREAD BASKET

NAPKIN HOLDER

TAPAS

ABOUT 4½ FEET

COAT RACK UNDER THE TABLE (ALTHOUGH SAUCE SOMETIMES DRIPS ON THE CLOTHES.)

IT WAS ADRIENNE (WHO HAD INTRODUCED MY WORK TO A WHOLE BUNCH OF HIGHER-UPS AT LA CENTRAL) WHO LOVED THIS PLACE AND HAD BROUGHT US HERE.

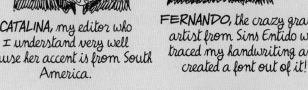

AT THIS POINT, I AM GOING TO DRAW THE PEOPLE WITH WHOM I ATE TO GIVE YOU SOME CONTEXT:

SCRATCH SCRATCH

The best I can...

Geez whiz, I can't draw women.

REGINA, my super-interpreter who I never went far without.

CATALINA, my editor who I understand very well because her accent is from South America.

FERNANDO, the crazy graphic artist from Sins Entido who traced my handwriting and created a font out of it!

JESÚS, the head of Sins Entido, who is also an architect and layout designer for Madrid's top expositions.

ADRIENNE, who is a food critic, meaning, she knows a lot about restaurants.
(WWW.GASTRONOMICAN.COM)

ENRIQUE, an architect and artist who also introduced my work to La Central. He has the real Spanish allure (but he's nice).

SHELIA, who takes care of a bunch of things at Sins Entido.

At La Casa Del Abuelo, we eat very well, and we can even send postcards to anywhere on the planet for free!

I'm going to write one to myself so that I can get a postcard from Spain.*

*SORRY, FRIENDS. I WASN'T IN THE MOOD TO LOOK UP YOUR ADDRESSES.

I stuff myself to the brim with olives, peanuts, and shrimp, and I'm soaking it up with all the bread that I can eat when Catalina announces that we are now going to eat dinner for real. It's 11pm.

Oh really? But um... no tengo miedo*

(Afraid? Afraid of what?)

No um... Mmm mmm yuck!

¿HAMBRE?

Hmm, yes, soy un hombre!

WHERE THE DEVIL IS REGINA?

*I ALWAYS CONFUSE HUNGER (HAMBRE) AND FEAR (MIEDO). I SHOULD FIGURE OUT WHY.

AT THE RESTAURANT

VIÑA P.

[3 PLAZA DE SANTA ANA]

WELL, LET ME JUST SAY THAT IT WAS SO GOOD THAT I ATE EVERYTHING, EVEN THOUGH I WASN'T HUNGRY ANYMORE:

Pimientos de Padrón

(fried mild mini peppers)

Carne roja (buey) a la piedra

Mayo, I think

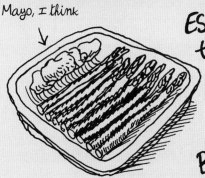

Espárragos trigueros

Grilled young green asparagus

(Amazing beef cooked in a well-oiled stone bowl).

Like having a table-side barbeque.

Berenjenas fritas

Fried eggplant

patatas fritas (Basically, good fries)

Crema Castellana (A type of crème brûlée with nuts)

THE PROBLEM IS THAT WE'RE DRINKING A LOT OF WINE (THAT WOULD NOT REALLY BE A PROBLEM IF I DIDN'T HAVE TO GET UP AT 9 A.M. THE NEXT DAY) AND WE'RE ALSO DRINKING THIS:

↙ ORUJO DE HIERBAS

PACHARÁN (SLOE BRANDY MADE OUT OF LOCAL PLUMS)

ORUJO BLANCO

ORUJO IS, FROM WHAT I UNDERSTAND, MADE FROM THE DISTILLED GRAPE SKINS. BUT AFTER THREE GLASSES, I DON'T UNDERSTAND MUCH ANYMORE.

(Should we have one last drink?)

(W...What? You're not tired?)

(It's only 2 A.M.!)

(Haha, more than seven hours of sleep!)

WE HAVE ONE LAST DRINK AT

museo chicote

(12 GRAN VÍA) THAT IS A RATHER HYPED-UP PLACE THAT HEMINGWAY USED TO FREQUENT, OR SO THEY SAY.

(In Spain, gin and tonics have been all the rage for the past two years.)

(Shit, $11 for a gin and tonic?)

(You'd think we're in Paris.)

(Oh, that's not bad!)

THE MENU IS EXCLUSIVELY GIN AND TONICS. THERE MUST HAVE BEEN THIRTY KINDS. I LET CATALINA CHOOSE FOR ME.

AS IT TURNS OUT, $11 GIN AND TONICS ARE NOT ACTUALLY EXPENSIVE...

Ooh man yo puedo barely lift it!

Yo am going to die!

(Pepper, citrus zest, gin, tonic)

...BECAUSE THE COCKTAILS WE ARE SERVED ARE AT LEAST A PINT EACH.

AFTER DRINKING HALF OF MY ~~GOBLET~~ GLASS,
I DON'T REMEMBER EXACTLY WHAT HAPPENED.

I THINK CATALIA SAID:

*IN COMICS, SPANISH SPEAKERS LAUGH LIKE
THIS. IT'S PRONOUNCED "RARA." I BEGIN
GOING ON ABOUT A THEORY ON LAUGHTER
AND DRINKING AND HOW THE TWO SHOULD
BE LINKED, SINCE "JAJA" BASICALLY MEANS
"ROWDY…"

THEN I LET IT GO. I EAT
TONS OF KIKOS TO SOAK THINGS
UP. THE COCKTAIL SNACK THAT
I LOVE, ALONG WITH CASHEWS

GRILLED AND SALTED CORN KERNELS… I'LL HAVE TO REMEMBER TO BUY SOME TOMORROW.

You also got a wild boar that you had sent to your parents... The taxidermist was really glad to have been woken up.

GOD-DAMN IT!

AND YOU DIDN'T STOP ME?

Nooo, you were funny!

Drunk, but funny.

THIS IS A CATASTROPHE. MY BANK IS GOING TO KILL ME.

an overdraft of $8,200 at... BEJAR. Who's this...the front man of Destroyer?

And suddenly

N...No... I can explain everything!

A BADGER, A BOAR... IT'S LIKE WE'RE IN AN **ANOUK RICARD** COMIC. SHIT.

We have breakfast at...

OLIVIa Te Cuida *

(8, santa teresa)

*(OLIVIA TAKES CARE OF YOU).

(IF YOU'RE GOOD!)

TE C[...]

¡JIJI!

Understanding the double meaning in Spanish

AT OLIVIA'S, THE AMBIANCE LIKE A SHABBY-CHIC SONOMA. WOOD AND TABLES, OLD BISTRO PARQUET FLOORS, AND IS ORGANIC-CHIC, WILLIAMS & STAINLESS STEEL CHAIRS, ANCIENT TOASTERS WITH THEIR EXTENSION CORDS CLIMBING TO THE CEILING. HIPSTER IN ITS OWN RIGHT, THE PLACE IS

"COZY".

I ORDER A FRUIT PLATTER AND A COFFEE BECAUSE I'M NOT VERY HUNGRY AFTER THE BLOW ABOUT THE BADGER (AND ALL THE KIKOS). I TALK TO THE JOURNALIST...

My perception of the distribution of Michelin macarons in Asia in light of [...]ening... No, I [...]te comics.

CO. MICS.

OLIVIA (OR SOME OTHER WOMAN) BRINGS ME THIS:

IN ONE SITTING, I EAT THE EQUIVALENT OF A YEAR'S WORTH OF FRUIT, SINCE I BUY IT SO INFREQUENTLY. NONE OF IT'S IN SEASON, BUT IT'S GOOD.

I don't know if it's eating gooseberries in the winter or spending $8,300 on dead animals that sit so heavily in my stomach.

THIS WILL DO.

Dr. Kousmine

REGINE MAKES ME TASTE HER MUESLI, WHICH IS SO GOOD I ALMOST WANT TO DIVE IN.

WE VISIT THE MUSEO ABC DE DIBUJO E ILUSTRACIÓN (29 CALLE DE AMANIEL) WITH JESÚS.

Whaa...that's crazy. It looks like Anna Sommet's work but from 1923!

And that looks like Blexbolex!

And that's like Solotareff!

It's crazy how styles cycle through the decades!

USUALLY, I ONLY TALK ABOUT FOOD IN MY TRAVEL JOURNALS, BUT HERE I MAKE AN EXCEPTION FOR THIS INCREDIBLE PLACE THAT I WOULD RECOMMEND TO ANYBODY INTERESTED IN ART.

AROUND 3 O'CLOCK, WE TAKE ON THE SERIOUS STUFF BECAUSE YESTERDAY, I SAID THESE ILL-FATED WORDS TO A JOURNALIST:

(Madrid's food scene? Well, not horrible, right? So... I'm familiar with croquetas... I find them a little fatty... Oh yeah, and I once ate a cocido madrileño at the Museo del Jamón* but it was nothing to write home about!)

OOOOOOOh!!

*REGINA TELLS ME LATER THAT EATING A COCIDO AT THE MUSEO DEL JAMÓN IS A LITTLE LIKE EATING TEXAS BARBECUE AT APPLEBEE'S. OR NEW ENGLAND CLAM CHOWDER FROM LONG JOHN SILVER'S. YOU GET WHERE I'M COMING FROM.

O DEL JAMO

HERE I AM GOING OUT WITH CATALINA, JESÚS, ENRIQUE AND A NEW PERSON:

JAVIER VIDAL BENEYTO.

ENCHANTÉ.

I AM THE ESON OF JOSÉ VIDAL BENEYTO.

↑
(SPEAKS FRENCH)

↑
(OBVIOUSLY WELL-KNOWN)

A GOOGLE SEARCH A FEW DAYS LATER WOULD TEACH ME WHO JOSÉ VIDAL BENEYTO WAS:

Damn...a well-known Spanish thinker...founded "El País"... So why did I tell his son the joke about the monkey who walked into a bar?

A shiiiit...

WE ARE NOW GOING TO EAT THE BEST COCIDO MADRILEÑO IN THE CITY, AT LEAST ACCORDING TO JAVIER AND JESÚS, AT:

TABERNA DE LA DANIELA
CERVEZAS — COCIDOS — BESUGOS

(TABERNA DE LA DANIELA, 7 PLAZA DE JESÚS)

The cocido eez not for yoking

JAVIER WARNS.

The **COCIDO** takes place in three stages:

➊ THE SOUP

You begin by serving yourself the broth (in which the meat and the vegetables were cooked). Here, it's served with vermicelli noodles, but that's not required, per se.

It's pretty savory, and the aroma is rather delicate. I serve myself seconds and thirds.

On the table are onions and mini peppers marinated in vinegar. There's also bread with a kind of tomato sauce in case you're _very_ hungry:

➋ THE VEGETABLES

CROQUETTES MADE OF WHO-KNOWS-WHAT — CARROTS — CHICKPEAS — POTATOES — CABBAGE

We are served a dish for about fifty people, but the vegetables are well cooked and soaked in broth: delicious.

➌ THE MEAT

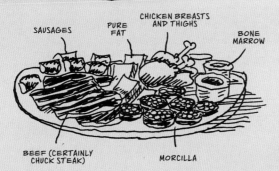

SAUSAGES — PURE FAT — CHICKEN BREASTS AND THIGHS — BONE MARROW

BEEF (CERTAINLY CHUCK STEAK) — MORCILLA

Was it good? Obviously. Did I eat too much of everything, especially the pure fat that reminded me of the taste of a real farm-raised pig? That, too. The moment is so perfect that I really want to believe that I am eating the best cocido in Madrid.

NEVERTHELESS, DURING THE MEAL I COMMIT A FAUX-PAS:

DON'T **EVER** ESERVE JOURSELF THE BROTH **WEETH** THE VEGETABLES OR THE MEAT, UNDERSTAND?

THEEZ EEZN'T THE CIRCUS, CABRÓN!

W-what if that's how I like it?

Oooh!

That kind of hurts, Javier.

(What did he do?)

(Gosh, these tourists.)

THE AMBIANCE IS NICE. THERE ARE AZULEJOS FROM EVERYWHERE ON THE WALLS, AND EVERYONE EATS WHILE TALKING NOISILY. WE'RE DRINKING A GOOD DEAL OF WINE IN ADDITION TO THE LITTLE WHITE AND GREEN DEVILS FROM LAST NIGHT THAT MAKE MY HEAD HURT:

COSME PALACIO CRIANZA 2008

SIX IN THE EVENING

AIR! GIVE ME AIR!! HELP!

I'VE GAINED SOME WEIGHT.

A LITTLE LATER, A MEETING AT THE INSTITUT FRANÇAIS FOR A COFFEE WITH NICOLAS, THE MAN IN CHARGE.

And you see, behind the wall there, we're in France! Otherwise, you've been happy with the food?

IN FRANCE!

It's fine, meh.

I'M GOING TO GET MYSELF DEPORTED IF I CONTINUE TO EAT LIKE THIS!

You know, for me, Madrid is really the best capital in Europe!

"THE KIND OF CITY WHERE GIRLS CAN WALK HOME AT THREE IN THE MORNING, WHERE DRUNK GUYS DON'T BOTHER EVERYONE LATE AT NIGHT. TO SAY NOTHING OF THE OVERALL KINDNESS OF THE PEOPLE."

Well, I'm saying this, and I read in the paper that yesterday an asshole tried to steal feathers from a peacock at the Casa de Campo around four A.M....

Hh...is that so?

Yep. Right??

Just goes to show there are weirdos everywhere.

Thankfully, there are security cameras in the park. They should be able to identify the guy pretty fast!

I'M GOING TO GO TO JAIL. I AM GOING TO BE BLACKLISTED BY INTERPOL... FUCK, ALL THIS BECAUSE OF A GIN AND TONIC...IN ADDITION TO THE OVERDRAFT ON MY BANK ACCOUNT!

I'M 35 YEARS OLD, AND MY LIFE IS OVER.

32456

Better keep a low profile.

In the evening, I meet with Marion*, a friend who is an editor at DIBBUKS:

*FRENCH

WE EAT (REASONABLE PORTIONS) AT A LITTLE DIVE THAT I TESTED OUT ON A PREVIOUS TRIP:

CISNE AZUL
19 CALLE DE GRAVINA

① TV TURNED ON (SOCCER) ② DISPLAY CASE OF ASSORTED MUSHROOMS ③ TABLE ④ POSTERS OF MUSHROOMS ⑤ COUNTER ⑥ SODA MACHINE

EL CISNE AZUL ISN'T CHEAP BUT YOU EAT VERY WELL, ESSENTIALLY FRESH MUSHROOMS. WE ORDER:

mezcla de setas ($15)

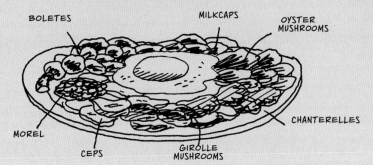

BOLETES · MILKCAPS · OYSTER MUSHROOMS · CHANTERELLES · GIROLLE MUSHROOMS · CEPS · MOREL

boletus con queso de cabra ($20)

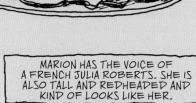

BOLETES · CHEESE

IT'S A LITTLE BIT EXPENSIVE FOR THE PLACE, BUT IT'S THE ONLY TIME I PAY FOR A MEAL THE ENTIRE TRIP, SO... THE MUSHROOMS ARE SAVORY, OBVIOUSLY, AND THE PORTIONS ARE GENEROUS. THE FOOD IS SIMPLE: A QUICK DIP IN OLIVE OIL, SALT AND PEPPER, AND DONE. IT'S THE BEST WAY TO DEAL WITH PRODUCTS THIS BEAUTIFUL.

MARION HAS THE VOICE OF A FRENCH JULIA ROBERTS. SHE IS ALSO TALL AND REDHEADED AND KIND OF LOOKS LIKE HER.

SO GOOD, RIGHT?

WANT TO SHARE THE MOREL?

IN THIS SETTING, I FEEL LIKE I'M IN ERIN BROCKOVICH.

JULIA MARION TALKS TO ME ABOUT A LOT OF THINGS: THE ECONOMIC CRISIS IN SPAIN, THE MORALE OF THE PEOPLE, THE FOOD SCENE, THE COST OF APARTMENTS... IN DISCUSSING MADRID'S NEIGHBORHOODS, I LEARN THAT...

So Malasaña is a district where you go to party. You know, Manu Chao sings about it in his song...

♪ Me gusta Malasaña Me gustas tú ♪

Ha, yeah of course!

I always thought he was saying "Me gusta la lasagna," and I couldn't understand why!

So, are you going to tell me what you're wearing a disguise? Is it because of the success of your book?

No, no, it's because of Hemingway.

Oh really?

No, but... I did some BAD things.

In life, or a...

Last night.

But um, you don't think that it will blow over?

I mean... you didn't kill someone or torture animals.

I don't want to talk about it.

How about one last dri...

No, we'd better not.

IT'S AROUND 1 A.M. WHEN I GET BACK TO THE HOTEL. FORGET GOING TO SLEEP AT A GOOD HOUR. I HAD TAKEN CARE OF THE STUFFED BADGER AND THE PEACOCK FEATHERS.

However, no way to remember if I actually ate at Burger King... I shouldn't blow this opportunity like I did in Stockholm.

Okay. One last thing and then to bed.

I have nothing to lose, and shit, everyone has the right to s...

*SEE TDTE 2.

CASA DE CAMPO, 3:40 A.M.

SORRY FOUR THE FEATHER. I DIDN'T WANT! HEAR THEY ARE.

P.S. DON'T LOOK FOR ME MORE I HAVE RETURNED TO MY COUNTRY CHINA

47

TODAY, THE SUN IS SHINING THROUGH MY WINDOW... AND MY HEART SADDENS AS I GAZE ACROSS THE CITY...

AH... MADRID.

I SHOULD EAT SOMETHING.

IT'S 8 A.M.... I DIDN'T SLEEP MUCH, SO I WALKED TO WHERE ALL HUNGRY WANDERING LOCALS GO IN THE MORNING...

EL DESTINO FUE QUIEN PUSO MÁS

Y TE ALEJA HOY DE MÍ

* IN MADRID, THE PEDESTRIAN LIGHT CHIRPS WHEN IT'S GREEN. DON'T ASK ME WHY.

chocolatería san Ginés

(11 PASADIZO SAN GINÉS)

THE PLACE IS KIND OF A CHEESY TEA HOUSE SLASH TOURIST TRAP, BUT I HAVE TO ADMIT THAT WHEN YOU ORDER THEIR MYTHICAL **"CHOCOLATE CON CHURROS"** FOR $4.50, YOU GET YOUR MONEY'S WORTH.

6 HOT AND CRUNCHY CHURROS

HOT CHOCOLATE TO DIE FOR

DAMN! THIS HOT CHOCOLATE IS AS DENSE AS A JAMES JOYCE NOVEL.

MY CHURROS CAN STAND STRAIGHT UP IN IT!

IF, LIKE ME, THE IDEA THAT YOU HAD OF CHURROS BEFORE NOW WAS:

HOT DOGS!

PEANUTS!

CHURROS! GET THEM WHILE THEY'RE

GO TO THIS CHOCOLATERÍA IN MADRID. IT'S A SACRED MOMENT OF GASTRONOMIC INDULGENCE.

WELL, ON THE OTHER HAND, I WOULDN'T GO THERE EVERY WEEK. ONCE A YEAR WOULDN'T BE TOO BAD.

I WANT TO GO FOR A SWIM TO HELP ME DIGEST, BUT I CAN'T FIND ANY BUSES HEADED TO THE BEACH. INSTEAD, I RENT A ROWBOAT AT THE LAKE IN EL RETIRO PARK, NOT FAR FROM DOWNTOWN...

I...RHH...I THINK I...'M BECOMING DIABETIC...

♪ ROW, ROW, ROW YOUR BOAT ♪

GENTLY DOWN THE STREAM ♪

SHLAF!

SHLAF!

SHLAF!

THE PLACE LOOKS MUCH BETTER THAN I CAN DRAW IT.

AT ONE MOMENT, CATALINA CALLS, BUT I DON'T PICK UP RIGHT AWAY BECAUSE I'M CONVINCED THAT IT'S INTERPOL, LOOKING FOR ME:

(AH... CATALINA? H... HOW DID YOU GET THIS NU...)

(NO, I DON... WHAT? WHAT MEETING?)

(OH YEAH, THAT'S RIGHT.)

OH SHIIT...

(NO NO, I'M ON MY WAY!)

IN FACT, I HAD COMPLETELY FORGOTTEN ABOUT A MEETING WITH HER, JESÚS, AND JAVIER AROUND 10 A.M. AT...

PESCADOS Y MARISCOS FERNANDO VI

GRAN PESCADERÍA Y MARISCOS · FERNANDO VI ·

GRAN

PESCADERIA

Pescadería fernando VI

(10 FERNANDO VI STREET)

JAVIER MAKES ME VISIT THE PESCADERÍA FERNANDO VI, THE PLACE WHERE, ACCORDING TO HIM, YOU FIND THE BEST OF THE SEA IN MADRID.

Ah well, okay, it's basically a fish mar—

NO. EETZ THE FEESH MARKET

WHATZ WEETH THEES LOOK?

Nothing, I uh... Tell me, do you have any contacts high up in the

JOU DON'T LOOK TOO BAD WITH A MUSTACHE, HOMBRE!

At the same time, since we're next to the ocean, it's like trying to find the best fish market in Boston.

YOU TALKEENG OR COMEENG?

Comeeng.

DING DONG

WE SEE:

PERCEBES
(GOOSENECK BARNACLES)
90€/KG

ALMEJAS (CLAMS) 30€/KG

COCOCHAS
(HAKE THROAT) 6€/KG

WHILE JAVIER GIVES ME THE INVENTORY OF THE STORE, I TRY TO GUESS WHAT HE IS GOING TO COOK FOR ME FOR LUNCH...

I would really like those gooseneck barnacles!

PESCADILLA PEQUEÑA
(SMALL WHITING) 11€/KG

LANGOSTINOS (SHRIMP)
39€/KG

HUEVAS (COD EGGS,
I THINK) 11€/KG

BESUGOS (RED SEA
BREAM) 30€/KG

SALMONETES DE ROCA
(STRIPED RED MULLET)
20€/KG

LENGUADOS MIGOSO
(SOLE) 24€/KG

AT ONE POINT, WE ALSO LOOK AT THE LOBSTERS IN A GLASS TANK:

LOOK EEN THE MEEDLE, ONE'S ALREADY COOKED... HE'S FOR FEEDING THE OTHERS!

Ooh...then Javier is going to make me a fucking lobster!

EXCEPT THAT...NOT AT ALL, ACTUALLY. NEITHER LOBSTER, NOR GOOSENECK BARNACLES, NOR RED SEA BREAM...

But we're jus lookeeng, right? These feesh are beautiful.

Oh, of course, sí.

(It's very super.)

AFTERWARD, WE VISIT A MARKET. STILL WITHOUT BUYING ANYTHING.

The **MERCADO BARCELÓ**, 6 Barceló Street (not at all an homage to the painter Barceló) is an architectural wonder conceptualized by Fuensanta Nieto and Enrique Sobejano. They remodeled the square and integrated a new market, an athletic center, and a preschool, all in relationship to the former historical market building.

THAT'S AT LEAST WHAT I UNDERSTAND A MONTH LATER WHILE RECOPYING AN AERIAL PHOTO OF THE MARKET FROM THE INTERNET.

They look like coffins!

That's cool!

BECAUSE IN THE MOMENT, ALL THAT I SEE IS THIS:

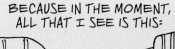

Wait, you want to make me visit this prefabricated rat hole?

INSIDE, EVERYTHING IS A LITTLE UGLY AND MODERN, WHICH DOESN'T MAKE ME WANT TO DRAW. HOWEVER, THE PRODUCTS ARE BEAUTIFUL, AND THE PLACE IS VERY BUSY.

Shit! Iberian Pata Negra ham for $27/lb!

¡Tonto! If you don't pay at least $60/lb, it's not the real thing.

OH REALLY, I SEE...

JAVIER TALKS TO ME OF HIS SPAIN OF THE
PEOPLE, WHICH IS BECOMING HARDER TO FIND.
HE SAYS IT'S GIVING WAY LITTLE BY LITTLE TO
HYPED-UP PLACES AND HIPSTER NEIGHBORHOODS.
THE GENTRIFICATION SEEMS TO ME TO BE
RATHER RECENT, WHICH CONTRASTS STRANGELY
WITH SPAIN'S FINANCIAL CRISIS.

(BUDDING POLITICAL CONSCIOUSNESS)

HOWEVER, THE CRISIS, GLOBALIZATION,
AND THE MONTH OF JANUARY DON'T PREVENT
ME, IN THE VEGETABLE SECTION*, FROM
ASKING ASK JAVIER TO CHOOSE ME
"A FUCKING GOOD TOMATO."

CATALINA AND
JESÚS ARE
WITH US, BUT
I DON'T HAVE
ENOUGH SPACE
TO DRAW THEM.

WELL...IS IT BECAUSE JAVIER IS
WATCHING ME? IS IT BECAUSE
I AM FRUSTRATED ABOUT THE
BARNACLES? OR IS IT BECAUSE
I'M MEGA-ASHAMED OF EATING A
TOMATO IN WINTER AND FINDING IT
DELICIOUS? WHO KNOWS. BUT
IT'S DEFINITELY A "FUCKING
GOOD TOMATO."

TASTE

PLUMP

BEAUTY

JUICE

*THE MARKET IS ACTUALLY DIVIDED
INTO "SECTIONS": CHEESE,
VEGETABLES, MEAT, ETC.

AFTER THE MARKETS, JESÚS TAKES
CONTROL OF THE SITUATION:

(WELL, MAYBE WE STOP
EYEING UP ZUCCHINI AND
GO HAVE A DRINK?)

WE GO HAVE A DRINK AT

Santa Barbara

8 SANTA BÁRBARA SQUARE

I meeeeed you... Baby please... Baby, baby, baby, babyyyy please... ♪

FOR THOSE UNDER THE AGE OF 25, I ADORE THIS SONG FROM SANTA BARBARA, AN AWESOME SERIES (BETTER THAN GAME OF THRONES OR BREAKING BAD, YOU SHOULD ~~DOWNLOAD~~)

NATURALLY, WHEN THE BEER ARRIVES, I AM HANDED THE LARGEST GLASS TO MY DISPLEASURE:

(A LOT! GOOD, MMM.)

(HAHA, I T'S GOOD, RIGHT?)

NOTE TO SELF: DON'T EVER SHOW THEM MY PIECE ON BREWERS.

WITH THE BEERS, THANKFULLY WE ORDER SHRIMP AND CHIPS:

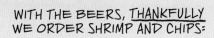

CHILLED UNSEASONED SHRIMP

FANTASTIC CHIPS

"Those were the days, my friend" ♪

Come here ONLY for the chips or the shreemp...the menu has become a mess. They even eserve paella!

IT'S A BEER HALL, MEANING, YOU DRINK BEER THERE. GREAT.

IN SPAIN, THERE IS A WHOLE TRADITION AROUND BEER. FIRST OF ALL, THE POURING:

TIRAR LA CAÑA: *(According to my understanding)*

Ⓐ RINSE THE BEER GLASS

② TILT THE GLASS 45 DEGREES AND POUR FROM THE TAP

③ TILT THE GLASS BACK UP WHEN THE BEER APPROACHES THE RIM

④ ALLOW THE BEER TO FOAM AT LEAST 8MM SO THAT THE BUBBLES IN THE BEER DON'T ESCAPE

ESPUMA

BURBUJAS

↕ 8MM

WHEN YOU DRINK THE CAÑA, EACH SIP LEAVES A WHITE CIRCLE ON THE GLASS. THIS IS CALLED A **TRAGO.**

BEER LOVER: 4 OR 5 TRAGOS AND IT'S DONE.

ME: AROUND 15 TRAGOS AS I CHOKE IT DOWN.

DÉCOR FROM THE 19TH CENTURY

AFTERWARDS, WE GO TO ANOTHER
PLACE FOR ANOTHER DRINK. THAT'S
THE PRINCIPLE OF TAPAS, IN SHORT.

BURP

BEEP

↑
TEXT MESSAGE

Shiiiiit

FROM MOMMY:
HI ~~SWEETIE~~ WE
RECEIVED A
DELIVERY NOTICE FOR
A PACKAGE FROM
SPAIN. IS
IT FROM
YOU? SHOULD
WE KEEP IT?

No choice.

FROM GIGI:
NO. DON'T ACCEPT
THE PACKAGE.
REMEMBER ANTHRAX
IN 2001? I DIDN'T
SEND ANYTHING.
OTHERWISE,
THE WEATHER'S
FINE.
XXOO

yes!

FROM MOMMY:
ANTHRAX??? I'LL
ALERT THE POSTAL
SERVICE AND HAVE
THEM DESTROY
THE PACKAGE! MY
GOD, TERRORISTS!
AND TO THINK THAT
I BELIEVED...

WE DROP BY AN EXCELLENT...SARDINIAN...RESTAURANT
CALLED:

La Tavernetta
(17, CALLE DE ORELLANA)

ALBERTO LOI
NIBARU

MORTADELLA (I LOVE THIS
SO MUCH THAT ONE DAY I'LL
WRITE A STORY ABOUT IT)

I think I'm going
to die from an
overdose of
satisfaction*

COPPA + LEMON
AND OLIVE OIL

(*COPYRIGHT
SALVADOR DALI)

GREEN
OLIVES

EVERYTHING IS <u>REALLY</u>
GOOD. EVERYTHING WAS
FREE, I MEAN, I THINK SO,
SINCE JAVIER
KNOWS THE OWNER*:

Hey! The one who loves
Sardinian tomatoes!
Into my arms!

*HE JUST READ
TDTE 1.

AND THERE'S
EVEN A DEESH WEETH
MY NAME ON IT!

"BUSIATI
CON RAGUT
DE COSTILLAS
DE CERDO
IBÉRICO"
(POR JAVIER
VIDAL)

54

AROUND 3 P.M., WE GO OUR SEPARATE
WAYS. I SAY GOODBYE TO JAVIER
AND JESÚS, AND WITH CATALINA, WE GO HAVE
A FINAL BITE BEFORE MY FLIGHT.

IT BEGINS TO RAIN.
YOU'D THINK WE WERE IN A MOVIE.

Umbrellas
are tough
to draw!

No such luck. Foiled again.
Cataline takes me for a bite at:

Juana La Loca
(4 PUERTA DE MOROS SQUARE)

Historically speaking, this bar is about her. (She doesn't look crazy, right?)

THE BAR IS JAM-PACKED. DESPITE WHAT MY SPEECH BUBBLES SUGGEST, WE CAN BARELY HEAR OURSELVES TALK. I LOVE THIS PLACE... ON THE MENU, A LOT OF WORDS ARE SPELLED WITH "X." WE ARE DEFINITELY IN BASQUE COUNTRY.

(This is what you wanted, right?)

(Monarchy, fast, better than fast food.)

Let's leave it at that.

(Happy?)

MH.

CATALINA EXPLAINS THAT THIS PLACE HAS (IN HER OPINION) THE BEST TORTILLA OF MADRID, ALL WHILE ADMITTING THAT THERE ARE AS MANY BEST TORTILLAS IN MADRID AS THEY ARE MADRILENIANS. I WANT TO BELIEVE HER ANYWAY:

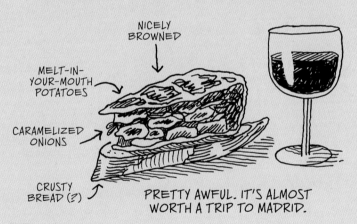

NICELY BROWNED

MELT-IN-YOUR-MOUTH POTATOES

CARAMELIZED ONIONS

CRUSTY BREAD (?)

PRETTY AWFUL. IT'S ALMOST WORTH A TRIP TO MADRID.

CATALINA TAKES ME TO THE AIRPORT, AND WE PROMISE TO SEE EACH OTHER AGAIN FOR THE SECOND VOLUME OF TO DRINK AND TO EAT.

(Did you enjoy your stay?)

(Yes, very much)

(Were you able to do everything yo

(Almost.)

(These are cars in the rain that I drew.)

MADRID-BARAJAS AIRPORT

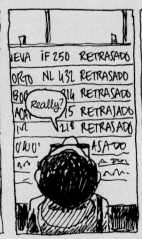

EVA IF250 RETRASADO
ORTO NL432 RETRASADO
800 814 RETRASADO
ACA 15 RETRAJADO
21 RETRASADO

Really?

Yeah, it's me. There's too much snow in Geneva for the airplane so...

Yeah, exactly.

Three-hour delay.

NO.

Yeah I'm fine.

MH

Yeah, I will have eaten.

Yes, Mommy, love you, too.

A THREE-HOUR WINDOW. IT IS GOING TO BE TIGHT, BUT I MAYBE CAN DO IT.

SORRY!

SORRY!

SORRY!

SORRY!

THIS SNOW IS MY SAVIOR. MY FREEDOM.

(CAN YOU TAKE ME TO MADRID?)

(YES, WHAT'S THE ADDRESS?)

BURGER KING.

ÉPILOGUE

GOOD LORD!

A BURGER KING!

(IMAGINE A SUPER WELL-DRAWN HORSE HERE.)

O noblest, the Burger King
Here I perceive your beef aflame
Your bun, your fries, my heart does ring
In hopes of finding you untamed
For you, I'd scale the highest peaks
Pierce through dark nights and bloody dread
I write your virtue in my dreams
To once more taste your fluffy bread.

In the Kingdom of Spain

CATACLOP CATACLOP

Bah, that doesn't work. I don't know how to do medieval...

What is this, The Princess Bride?

A let's start over.

IN THE TAXI FROM THE AIRPORT TO BURGER KING:

(HEY, PABLO, SEE THIS CREDIT CARD RIPPED IN HALF?)

(UM... YES, SIR?)

(THE OTHER HALF FOR YOU IF YOU LET MOTOR PLAY WHILE ME IN CITY WAIT.)

(O-OKAY, SIR.)

SO THIS IS HOW MY DREAM IS GOING TO COME TRUE. AFTER HAVING MISSED MY CHANCE IN STOCKHOM, I AM FINALLY GOING TO EAT AT BURGER KING AGAIN. I'VE WAITED 15 YEARS FOR THIS. THE TAXI IS NOT GOING TO EXPLODE, THE RESTAURANT WILL NOT BE CLOSED. I AM NOT GOING TO HAVE A STROKE.

It's almost too easy.

I can't believe it.

I GO INSIDE. THERE'S A GOOD MANY PEOPLE DESPITE THE WEATHER (WHY WOULD RAIN CHANGE YOUR APPETITE ANYWAY). MOSTLY TOURISTS, MANY OF THEM FRENCH AND GRINNING LIKE IDIOTS (PILGRIMS, LIKE ME).

HEYYY CHECK OUT THE GUY BEHIND ME.

BE LESS OBVIOUS.

WHO? MUSTACHE JOE?

WHATEV, HE DOESN'T SPEAK FRENCH.

HEH HEH HEH

YEAH, GUESS WHERE I'M CALLING FROM?

YAAAS!

I ORDER A TRIPLE WHOPPER MEAL AND A COKE (A-COLA). I PINCH MYSELF TO MAKE SURE THAT I'M NOT DREAMING.

(A) I FIRST EAT THE FRIES:

GRAMF! FOOD! MMM! CRUNCH!

THEY'RE NOT BAD. ACTUALLY, THEY'RE OKAY. I REMEMBER THEM BEING BETTER.

This can't be reaaaal!

BUT I'M NOT DREAMING. I JUST LOOK LIKE A CRAZY PERSON PINCHING HIMSELF IN A FAST FOOD RESTAURANT.

(2) I DRINK SOME COKE.

SLRRRRP! SLURP! BURP!

SOME FAST FOOD COKE, ICE CUBES OUT THE WAZOO.

GOOD.

ALL THIS FOR **NOTHING.**
AND TO THINK THAT I'VE
BEEN GOING ON ABOUT
THE LOSS OF BURGER KING
FROM FRANCE FOR
FIFTEEN YEARS...

LET'S BE CLEAR: IT'S NOT
ACTUALLY HORRIBLE. IT IS STILL
BETTER THAN MOST FAST-FOOD,
BUT... IT'S STILL FAST FOOD.
MEANING, IT'S NOT VERY GOOD.

And it's always the same when you compare the burger on TV with one in front of you...*

*READ CNBC'S "WHY RESTAURANT MEALS DON'T LOOK LIKE THE ADS."

Nogood, my ass! Fastfude, my ass!

You've just gotten older!

Hm!

?

TRIPLE WHOPPER

ALL THIS
UNFORTUNATELY
JUST CONFIRMS MY...

GROO

HUNGER
PANGS

CRAVING FOR SOME
GOOD FAST FOOD

Fast Food THEORY

Whose rules even apply to Burger King!

VICIOUS CYCLE

PRETEXT:
COMMERCIALIZED AREA,
HIGHWAY SERVICE PLAZA,
LACK OF TIME

FORGETFULNESS:
ONE TO SIX MONTHS
PASSES

PROMISE TO STOP
EATING FAST FOOD

IT'S
NOT
GOOD.

¡AL AEROPUERTO SIN DISCUTIR!

OBVIOUSLY, AFTER NOT HAVING TASTED IT IN FIFTEEN YEARS, MY DISAPPOINTMENT IS AS GREAT AS MY ANTICIPATION...I SWEAR TO NEVER AGAIN COMPLAIN ABOUT NOT HAVING BURGER KING IN FRANCE AND ~~TO NEVER AGAIN~~ TO EAT FAST FOOD LESS OFTEN.

WHILE WAITING FOR MY AIRPLANE IN THE TERMINAL, I RECEIVE TWO TEXTS FROM MY MOM: GENEVA IS STILL SNOWED IN.

~~SNUCKUMS~~, MAKE SURE YOU DON'T HAVE A SCAR NEAR YOUR KIDNEYS. YOU KNOW THAT ORGAN TRAFFICKING IS

I MADE A GOOSE AND AN ARTICHOKE THISTLE GRATIN WITH SOME ÎLE FLOTTANTE FOR DESSERT. WE'LL BE WAITING FOR YOU! PAPA'S SHUCKING OYSTERS FOR THE APPETIZER. KISSES.

INTERPOL, AT THE SAME TIME

THAT'S OUR GUY.

IT'S HE WHO PUT THE ANTHRAX IN

YES.

AND THE PEACOCK FEATHERS

THAT TOO.

WE'LL ARREST HIM IN GENEVA.

WHAT IF HE'S ARMED?

WE'LL BLOW UP THE PLANE.

INTERPOL

ON THE PLANE, I THINK AGAIN OF MY TASTE BUDS THAT HAVE LOST A LITTLE FAITH; OF THIS SPAIN THAT HAS LOST A LITTLE HOPE. I TRY TO FIND A PARALLEL BETWEEN THE TWO BUT COME UP WITH NOTHING.

WAS I WON OVER BY MADRID'S FOOD? ABSOLUTELY. WILL I GO BACK? CERTAINLY. IF MY PLANE DOESN'T EXPLODE MID-FLIGHT!

THIS IS YOUR CAPTAIN SPEAKING. THERE'S TOO MUCH SNOW, WE ARE GOING TO MAKE AN EMERGENCY LANDING.

HAAAAAA! AAAAA!

NAHH, JUST MESSIN', ALL GOOD!

WOOOOOOOOOO

BUT EVERYTHING GOES FINE. WE LAND PEACEFULLY. I AM GOING TO EAT MY THIRD DINNER IN ABOUT AN HOUR.

I WILL BE BACK.

leon.

Summer

Adrift

BARCELONA BEACH, MAY 2014

THE HEAT IS SO DIZZYING THAT I'VE LINGERED HERE OVER AN HOUR.

COME CLOSER... THERE. YOU SEE THE LITTLE DOT DISAPPEARING BETWEEN THE TWO WAVES NEAR THE HORIZON?

THAT'S ME.

I'M FLOATING TO TRY TO RELAX. I HAVE JUST EATEN NONSTOP FOR A WEEK. MY STOMACH RISES FROM THE WATER LIKE A SOFT LITTLE ISLAND.

I WAS INVITED BY MY SPANISH EDITOR TO THE SALÓ INTERNACIONAL DEL CÒMIC FOR THE RELEASE OF *A COMER Y A BEBER* VOLUME 2.

SINCE I BEGAN **TDTE**--THIS MASTERPIECE THAT HAS SINCE BECOME AN AUTHORITY IN THE CULINARY WORLD--I SOMETIMES HAVE THE FEELING THAT MY LIFE NOW REVOLVES AROUND ONLY ONE THING:

EATING.

OF COURSE, I CONSIDER MYSELF LUCKY: I CAN SAY THAT I HAVE A JOB THAT PUTS FOOD ON THE TABLE. LITERALLY.

EXCEPT SOMETIMES, LIKE NOW, I AM COMPLETELY SATURATED WITH FOOD.

GO AHEAD, SPOIL THE ENDING. IT'S TOO LATE FOR ME TO SEE IT, ANYWAY.

MEH, OK, HANG ON.

I THINK MY THROAT IS SEIZING UP... THE CONCEPT OF "EATING" SOUNDS TOTALLY FOREIGN TO ME.

I EXPERIENCE THE RARE FEELING (WELL, AT LEAST IN MY CASE) OF "THE OPPOSITE OF HUNGER."

ALL OF THE SUDDEN, HE SHOOTS A LASER PISTOL INTO IT AND THE CAVE BEGINS TO MOVE!

OH YEAH?

YEP. AND THEN THEY ALL START FREAK-ING OUT.

I TRY NOT TO THINK OF THE TAPAS THAT ARE WAITING FOR ME OVER THERE, ON DRY LAND.

THEN, THEY GET BACK INTO THE SHIP AS FAST AS THEY CAN, AND THEY TAKE OFF.

AND THE GIRL SAYS, "THE CAVE IS COLLAPSING!"

OR OF THE WORK THAT REMAINS TO FINISH THE THIRD VOLUME OF TDTE.*

I REALLY HAVE TO STOP WRITING ABOUT FOOD.

AND HAN SOLO SAYS "THIS IS

GLPP!

SHIIT!

INSTEAD, I SHOULD WRITE THE SCIENCE-FICTION COMIC THAT I'VE BEEN WANTING TO DO FOR YEARS.

OUTER SPACE... SEEMS LESS RISKY.

*THE VERY ONE THAT YOU HOLD IN YOUR HANDS THAT TREMBLE WITH EMOTION.

I SHOULD SAY... WELL BEFORE ~~MAKING IT BIG~~ WRITING ABOUT FOOD, I ALWAYS MADE AN EFFORT TO LIVE IN PLACES KNOWN FOR THEIR CUISINE.

24 BOXES "KITCHEN"

3 BOXES "CLOTHES + MISC."

AS SOON AS WE GET THERE, WE'LL EAT, 'KAY?

GENEVA, FIRST, WHERE I GREW UP...

ARBOIS.

AND FINALLY, LYON.

EVEN WHEN ON VACATION, I ALWAYS PRIORITIZED THE CHOICE OF RESTAURANTS OVER THE CHOICE OF HOTELS.

YOU WILL SEE THIS IMAGE AGAIN.

AND WHEN A DESTINATION SPEAKS TO ME, IT'S USUALLY OUT OF CULINARY CURIOSITY.

LET'S SEE... RUSSIA, MEH.

AH.

VIETNAM.

MMM

NOT THE UNITED STATES...

ASIA... SOUTH-EAST.

SINCE *TO DRINK AND TO EAT,* I HAVE BECOME, DESPITE MYSELF, "SOMEONE WHO KNOWS SOMETHING" ABOUT FOOD.

LAUGHS AT HIS OWN JOKES

Huhhuh huh!

STORY IN PROCESS

NESCAFÉ INSTANT COFFEE

THE FACT THAT I'M OFTEN MISTAKEN FOR A JOURNALIST (I WORK FOR THE FRENCH NEWSPAPER LEMONDE.FR) AND I'M ALSO PUBLISHED IN FRANCE BY GALLIMARD (A BIG DEAL) SURELY CONTRIBUTES TO THIS.

YOU'LL SEE, IT'S LITERALLY THE LAND MEETS THE SEA! THEY MAKE A BLEND OF FL... I LOV...OW ...TURE

UM YEAH B...

WELL, YOU TELL ME!

YOU'RE THE EXPERT, AFTER ALL!

YEAH...

AT RESTAURANTS, PEOPLE OFTEN WAIT FOR MY COMMENTARY OR REACTION...

SO? HM?

HANG ON 'IS HOH!

ISN'T IT TO DIE FOR?

YOU TAST' THE NOTE OF SICHU PEPPER

RIGHT?

...THE TRUTH IS THAT I DON'T KNOW MUCH ABOUT ANYTHING.

I'M LIKE MOST PEOPLE: EITHER IT'S NOT GOOD, IT'S GOOD, OR IT'S EXCELLENT.

WELL, I DUNNO... WHAT DO YOU THINK?

IT'S NOT HMM. IT'S EXCELLENT.

A WELL-KNOWN

Y...YEAH. EXACTLY. DITTO.

THE SALMON MARRIES PERFECTLY

LET THE READER BE ASSURED THAT I STILL KNOW HOW TO RECOGNIZE AN ALMAS CAV...

WAIT A MINUTE...

SHIT, SO I CAN'T DRAW A SCIENCE-FICTION COMIC?

THIS THING IS STILL ABOUT FOOD!

WELL.

WHERE WAS I AGAIN?

OH, THERE YOU ARE! WEIRDO.

THAT'S RIGHT. THE SEA.

B-GNET,... ONE OF THE FRENCH AUTHORS INVITED TO THE FESTIVAL.

SHIT MAN, WE WERE LOOKING FOR YOU EVERYWHERE! YOU COMING?

UH... WHY?

WHAT DO YOU MEAN, WHY?

IT'S THE LAST EVENING OF TAPAS WITH THE PUBLISHERS AND THE WHOLE WORKS!

OH, THAT.

SO, UM... ARE YOU HUNGRY?

A STRONG MORCILLA AT THE BEGINNING OF THE WEEK HAD SENT A FATAL BLOW TO HIS STOMACH.

HAHA! NOT AT ALL, BUT I'M GOING TO PRETEND TO EAT.

OH OKAY.

I'M GETTING PRETTY GOOD AT IT.

SO... SOONER OR LATER, I'LL HAVE TO FACE RETURNING TO DRY LAND...

OKAY... LET'S FLOAT ANOTHER FIVE MINUTES AND THEN GO?

TAKE YOUR TIME!

DON'T WORRY. IT WILL BE FINE.

...AND LEAVING BEHIND THIS ENCHANTED MOMENT OF CALM.

RETURN TO WORKING. RETURN TO EATING.

BECAUSE MY MOM OFTEN TOLD ME WHEN I WAS A KID:

"EAT."

"BECAUSE YOU NEVER KNOW WHAT WILL EAT YOU."

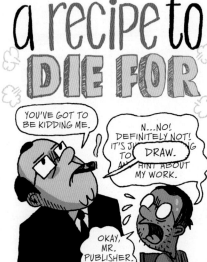

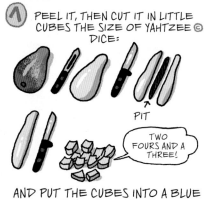

THE OTHER DAY, I WAS IN THE MIDDLE OF WATCHING CUTE CAT VIDEOS ON YEWTUBE IN ORDER TO RESEARCH A STORY.

HA!

"loop of kittens on a slide"

That's great!

Beginning in three, two, one:

clic!

AT THAT MOMENT, ONE OF THOSE AWFUL COMMERCIALS BEGAN PLAYING-- YOU KNOW, THE ONES THAT YOU HAVE TO PUT UP WITH FOR FIVE SECONDS. IT WAS THE ELEVEN THOUSANDTH TIME THAT I'D HEARD IT:

YOU HEARD RIGHT. OUR BEST APPETIZERS ARE NOW

Endless.

shit

GARLIC BASI

toast

ENDLESS. BUFFALO WINGS? THAT'S RIGHT

my ass

FOR A VERY LIMITED TIME, EACH PERSON'S PICK OF...

POF

...ONE OF OUR BEST, APPETIZERS IS ENDLESS. SO IF YOU'VE GOT TEN BUCKS YOU'RE IN. AND THE PARTY KEEPS GOING ALONG

Reheated

I DECIDED TO ACT.

We don't care.

I don't care if they have loaded fries. This commercial has ruined my afternoon!

Meow

Purr

BY SUGGESTING A RECIPE FOR AN APPETIZER THAT ACTUALLY TASTES GOOD.

It's easy to make and is perfect for summer!

sardine BUTTER

I'll even teach you a thing or two about sardines...

But nothing about butter, sorry!

Made with

salt and pepper

butter

a tin of sardines

fresh sardines

seaweed flakes

truffle oil

sweet or smoked paprika

scissors

bread

basil

lemon

whatever else suits your fancy.

First, you start with the sardines because it's a sardine butter, and for those, you have two options.

The easiest is to open a tin of...

of?

Sardines. Good job to those who were following.

CHOOSE FIRM ONES PACKAGED IN OLIVE OIL. WITH OR WITHOUT BONES--NOBODY CARES. IF THE FISHING DATE IS INDICATED, TRY TO GET SOME FROM OCTOBER. THEY WILL BE PLUMPER.

because I'm fat! I'm fat!

come on!

really really fat

who's fat!

FUN FACT: THE SARDINE TIN WAS INVENTED AT THE BEGINNING OF THE 19TH CENTURY, BUT THE PULL TAB FOR OPENING IT WASN'T INVENTED UNTIL FIFTY YEARS LATER.

Say, Edward, how are the sardines coming along?

Give me twenty more minutes.

Why can't this thing open like a can of Coke?

DINK! DINK!

① DRAIN THE SARDINES AS BEST YOU CAN:

(I'M DRAWING THREE BECAUSE IT TAKES UP LESS SPACE.)

② PUT THEM IN A BOWL AND ADD 4-6 TABLESPOONS OF SOFTENED BUTTER.

THEN BEGIN MIXING AND SMASHING THE SARDINES WITH A FORK.

③ ADD TO THE MIXTURE THE JUICE OF 1/2 TO 1 LEMON:

HMM... COULDN'T WE HAVE MORE SPECIFIC MEASUREMENTS?

THIS SUCKS.

IMPROVISE ACCORDING TO YOUR TASTE. WE'RE NOT IN A COOKBOOK, HERE. THE MIXTURE SHOULD BASICALLY HAVE THE CONSISTENCY OF CHICKEN SALAD:

GOOD.   NOT GOOD.

④ THAT'S IT. SEASON WITH SALT AND PEPPER, ADD SOME PAPRIKA OR SOME TRUFFLE OIL, FRESH BASIL, SEAWEED FLAKES, OR WHATEVER ELSE SUITS YOUR FANCY.

Hold up, young man! The dash of seaweed was my idea! And chuck the lemon, now that's a good boy.

← SONIA EZGULIAN, COLLECTOR OF SARDINE TINS

THEN, PUT IT INTO THE FRIDGE FOR ABOUT AN HOUR AND SERVE WITH SOME BREAD:

Mmmmm: itch delichious! But I see you're already asking: "What's the second method?"

It takes a little longer.

haha!

Change of scenery.

SNAP!

IMAGINE. YOU'RE ON VACATION WITH SOME FRIENDS A THOUSAND MILES FROM CIVILIZATION. ONE FRIEND -- LET'S CALL HIM "OLIVER"-- JUST DROVE AN HOUR FOR:

I bought six pounds of sardines so you can make us your famous butter with the leftove—

Didn't they have any in tins?

NO

Ah

Are they gutted?

NO.

Ah

Do we have to?

YES, YOU HAVE TO. BUT NO WORRIES, IT'S PRETTY EASY. AND PRETTY GROSS, BUT, ALL THE SAME, THIS ISN'T A RECIPE FOR CARROT BUTTER, NOW, IS IT?

① TAKE A PAIR OF SHARP SCISSORS AND A SARDINE:

NOTE THAT AT THIS STEP TO CHOOSE A GOOD SARDINE, IT HAS TO BE IN SEASON (FROM JUNE TO NOVEMBER). MAKE SURE THAT IT'S SHINY, FIRM, BRIGHT-EYED, AND WITHOUT A STRONG ODOR:

← A GOOD SARDINE

② WITH THE PAIR OF SCISSORS, CUT THE SARDINE ALONG THE DOTTED LINE:

ANUS   HEAD

IF THERE'S NOT A DOTTED LINE ON YOUR FISH, IMAGINE ONE. THEN GUT IT BY PULLING ON EVERYTHING THAT COMES OUT AND SEEMS GROSS:

WINTER IS COMING.

SCHLIPS!

YES. IT'S LIKE WATCHING AN EPISODE OF "GAME OF THRONES" AND BEING ONE OF THOSE PEOPLE FOR REAL.

③ RINSE THE INSIDE OF THE SARDINE WELL, THEN DO THE NEXT ONE, AND SO ON.

There you go! All that's left is to grill them and, tomorrow, take the leftovers, remove the filets, and make the sardine butter like explained before!

It's almost even better

IT'S PRETTY GREAT AS AN APPETIZER OR TO SERVE WITH COCKTAILS:

Yeah, this is a nice change from wings, for sure

Hey, I saw that for a limited time, everyone can get endless apps at

haaah on uioiii

ENJOY!

lon.

death bye lobstr

This is where texting is taking our spelling!

WHEN I WAS A KID, MY PARENTS AND I USED TO GO TO CORSICA OVER SUMMER VACATION WITH AN UNCLE WHO KNEW THE GULF OF SANTA MANZA, NORTH OF BONIFACIO, LIKE THE BACK OF HIS HAND.

ONE SUMMER, WE WERE EXPLORING CAP CORSE ON THE NORTHERN PART OF THE ISLAND. THE FIRST EVENING, WE STOPPED AT A KIND OF PIZZERIA THAT ALSO SERVED FISH AND SOME SPECIALTIES FROM SAVOY, BUT THERE WASN'T ANYTHING BETTER NEARBY.

MY PARENTS ORDERED SOME MACKEREL, BUT THE WAITRESS, DISTRESSED ABOUT A DISASTROUS DAY OF FISHING, SUGGESTED THE RED MULLET. GOOD SIGN. AS FOR ME, I ORDERED A LOBSTER WITH SPAGHETTI FOR 70 FRANCS (ABOUT 13 DOLLARS), BECAUSE THIS WAS A GOOD OPPORTUNITY TO HAVE SOME (BY THAT I MEAN THE LOBSTER).

WHILE WE WAITED FOR OUR MEALS, MY MOM JOKED THAT I'D LIKELY BE EATING SPAGHETTI WITH LOBSTER AT THAT PRICE. SHE SAID THAT IT DIDN'T MATTER, THAT I'D HAVE A GOOD EXPERIENCE, AND SHE WOULDN'T EVEN HAVE TO HELP ME SHELL IT.

WHEN THE WAITRESS CAME BACK A GOOD HALF HOUR LATER (A VERY GOOD SIGN), SHE PLACED IN FRONT OF MY PARENTS A DISH OF FRESH, GRILLED RED MULLET AND SOME GRILLED BREAD.

WITH THE SAME GESTURE, SHE PUT IN FRONT OF ME A ROASTED LOBSTER SPLIT IN TWO, ACCOMPANIED BY A SIMPLE DISH OF SPAGHETTI SEASONED WITH OLIVE OIL, GARLIC, AND A LITTLE RED PEPPER.

YEARS LATER, THIS EVENING STILL RANKS AMONG ONE OF MY GREATEST CULINARY EXPERIENCES.

I OFTEN ASK MY PARENTS IF THEY REMEMBER THE LOCATION OF THIS PLACE SO THAT I CAN GO BACK THERE SOMEDAY, BUT CLEARLY, THEIR RED MULLET WASN'T AS MEMORABLE AS MY LOBSTER. ALSO, WITH TIME, THIS HOLE IN THE WALL HAS LIKELY BECOME A REST STOP. WE CONSOLE OURSELVES AS WE CAN.

lon.

Today, I've been invited to my friend Fanny's house and she has made me a...

DING DONG

Chilled Zucchini Soup
With Feta

Heyy Fan!

Hey, why are you drawing me with my glasses?

Well I uh~

I'd prefer you didn't.

Mmm, that looks good

Oh, it was nothing, really easy.

I hope it's good.

TCHAK TCHAK TCHAK

ASIDE: LIKE SOME OF MY FRIENDS, FANNY SUFFERS FROM "TO DRINK AND TO EAT SYNDROME," MEANING THAT SHE THINKS I'M A CULINARY EXPERT BECAUSE OF MY COMICS. THIS MEANS THAT SHE ALSO THINKS THAT ANYTHING SHE MAKES ME COULDN'T BE GOOD ENOUGH FOR MY PALATE (EVEN THOUGH WE KNOW EACH OTHER WELL).

Here you gooo... Well, it doesn't look so nice, does it

Give it here.

TO MAKE THIS DISH, YOU WILL NEED (FOR, LET'S SAY, TWO PEOPLE):

2 OR 3 BEAUTIFUL ZUCCHINI

CREAM CHEESE (YEP)

SOME FETA

OLIVE OIL

PEPPER

SALT

MINT

① PEEL THE ZUCCHINI (WHILE LEAVING A LITTLE SKIN IF THEY'RE ORGANIC):

THEN CUT THEM INTO ROUNDS. TOSS INTO A SAUCEPAN, COVER WITH WATER, AND LET COOK AT LOW HEAT FOR 10–15 MINUTES (ROUGHLY):

② REMOVE FROM HEAT AND LET IT COOL COMPLETELY. ADD A TABLESPOON OR TWO OF CREAM CHEESE (YEAH, YEAH), A DOZEN MINT LEAVES (APPROXIMATELY):

AND MIX WITH AN IMMERSION BLENDER:

BVRRR RRRV

③ PUT THE SOUP IN THE FRIDGE FOR SEVERAL HOURS, THEN SERVE IN GLASSES (I DIDN'T SAY MASON JARS) WITH SOME DICED FETA. SEASON WITH SALT AND PEPPER, AND ADD A DRIZZLE OF OLIVE OIL:

Normally it's a lot better. Hey, you're not goi to talk about it on your blog

Mhm

Okay

no no

BOUFFE BOUFFE

And... Hey, head's up, the coffee's only Nespresso, okay?*

You're not going to like it

Cool.

* ANOTHER SYMPTOM OF THE TDTE SYNDROME.

leon.

NO, I'M GOING TO TELL YOU ABOUT:

pork ribs with "Kulisutofu" sauce

(IT'S CALLED THAT BECAUSE CHRISTOPHER IS CRAZY ABOUT THIS SAUCE, AND BECAUSE IN JAPANESE HIS NAME IS PRONOUNCED LIKE THAT. BUT THAT'S TOO MUCH TO EXPLAIN HERE.)

NOTHING'S EASIER THAN THIS MARINADE. YOU'LL NEED:

NEXT, FINELY DICE THE GARLIC. USE TWO CLOVES FOR EVERY FOUR PORK RIBS:

REMOVE THE GERM, OF COURSE.

IN THE FREEZER BAG (MUCH MORE PRACTICAL THAN A PLATE FOR DISTRIBUTING THE MARINADE), PUT:

AND LET THE RIBS MARINATE FOR AN HOUR OR SO, THE TIME TO HAVE ~~A BEER~~ A DRINK AND MAKE THE SAUCE.

Pépé Roni's Good Advice: flambé n° 758

Don't confuse "flamber"

And "flambé"

BECAUSE ANYONE CAN MAKE MISTAKES!

Flambé: To dress or serve a food doused with alcohol and set aflame.

Fall

I REALLY LIKE AUTUMN. THE SEASON IS A DREAM COME TRUE FOR FOODIES: YOU CAN STILL FIND SUMMER VEGETABLES, BUT YOU CAN ALSO GET SQUASH, MUSHROOMS, AND CABBAGE...

HEY, MUSHROOMS THAT I DON'T RECOGNIZE!

LOOK GOOD TO ME!

← HAS NEVER GONE MUSHROOM-PICKING.

AND APPLES.

APPLES ARE SO COOL. YOU CAN EAT THEM STRAIGHT FROM THE TREE, JUST AS THEY ARE.

GEECH   CHOMP   DELICH!   CHOMP

I'VE ALWAYS WANTED TO TALK ABOUT APPLES IN TO DRINK AND TO EAT.*

I BEGAN MAKING A LIST OF APPLES, BUT I DON'T KNOW THAT MANY OF THEM.

PINK LADY (MY FAVORITE)   REINETTE GRISE (FOR COOKING)   GRANNY SMITH (VERY TART, FOR SNACKING)

GALA (FREED FROM DESIRE)   GOLDEN DELICIOUS (BARF)   FUJI (NOT BAD)

AFTER THINKING ABOUT IT, I REALIZE I DON'T REALLY KNOW WHAT TO SAY ABOUT APPLES.

I WANTED TO DO A STORY ABOUT WILLIAM TELL:

OH SHIT, WALTER?   YOU OK?

TH..THERE'S SOME TARTE TATIN LEFT IF YOU WANT!

WALTER?

BUT... NOT GREAT.

I TOYED WITH THE IDEA OF NEWTON...

GOSH, DARN IT!   YOU DARE STRIKE ME WITHOUT GRAVITY?   I SHALL EAT YOU IN A GRANITA!

IN SHORT, HISTORICAL COMICS AREN'T REALLY MY THING.

I EVEN WORKED ON A STORY ABOUT THE CULINARY VERSION OF ROBERT CRUMB:

OH-Hey

BOB CRUMB

BUT IT WAS A LITTLE TOO, UMM...

aaag-HAHH!

...TOO MANY LITTLE LINES.

SO I DECIDED TO STICK WITH ME. IT SEEMED TO BE EASIEST.

THAT'S ME, THERE, FUC UH AN APPLE? YEAH?

YOU'RE A LITTLE SICK IN THE HEAD, MY BOY.

BUT... YOU... UH

IT WOULD BE BETTER TO DRAW YOURSELF, ESPECIALLY FOR THIS KIND OF THING.

DON'T IMPLICATE ME IN IT.

WHAT ARE YOU GETTING AT, ANYWAY?

TODAY, WE'RE TALKING...

*TDTE

A Bob Crumb crumble

GASP!
UH... I ACTUALLY THINK I'LL STICK AROUND.

Mm! Mm!

HURRY, MAN! DRAW ME!

IT'S ONE OF THE RARE DESSERTS, ALONG WITH CHOCOLATE CAKE*, THAT I HAVE MOSTLY MASTERED.

WHEN I STARTED MAKING IT, I CUT THE APPLES HOWEVER, GUESSED ON HOW MUCH FLOUR, SUGAR, AND BUTTER, AND THAT WAS IT!

THIRTY MINUTES IN THE OVEN, AND OUT CAME A VERY GOOD CRUMBLE!

MY **NEW FRIEND*** HELPED A LOT IN PERFECTING MY RECIPE:

What do you mean, "guessed" and "that was it!"

A crumble has rules.

Well, uhh...

Ah.

One fourth sugar, one fourth butter, and one half flour... unless you include almond flour or other stuff. In that case, it's one fourth flour and one fourth other stuff.

Writing this down?

Mentally

You'd better.

There are rules, shit.

YEARS PASSED, AND I IMPROVED MY CRUMBLE LIKE A TRUE CULINARY SCIENTIST...

What if I added a little sarsaparilla concentrate...

Screw the rules!

SHHHHH

HERE IS THE STATE OF MY RESEARCH ON THE ULTIMATE

APPLE

Dude, this is the second time you've written this fucking title!

ARE YOU HIGH?

NOPE.

JUST DISTRACTED.

YOU'RE BREAKING THE RULES!!

FIRST, YOU NEED APPLES. CHOOSING THE RIGHT APPLE IS VERY IMPORTANT. DEPENDING ON MY MOOD, I WORK WITH...

GRANNY SMITH FOR A TART, JUICY, AND TEXTURED CRUMBLE

BRAEBURN FOR A SWEET, JUICY, AND SUBTLE CRUMBLE

REINETTE GRISE FOR A SWEET, ALMOST BITTER, UNCTUOUS CRUMBLE

FIND THE APPLE THAT WORKS FOR YOU. ON SECOND THOUGHT, AVOID, IF POSSIBLE...

GOLDEN DELICIOUS!
BECAUSE IT'S BASICALLY JUST **SHIT!** IT'S FULL OF WATER AND HAS NO TASTE. NO SERIOUSLY, LET'S BE HONEST!

THE GOLDEN DELICIOUS IS THE McDONALDS OF APPLES!

JEAN-PIERRE COFFE →

← LEGITIMATE

LEADER PRICE

*READ TDTE 1.

PEEL, CORE, AND CUT THE APPLES. THE QUANTITY DEPENDS ON HOW MUCH OF THE OTHER INGREDIENTS YOU HAVE ON HAND:

Dude, cubing the apples is rather titillating! They're just so hard.

Hehe!

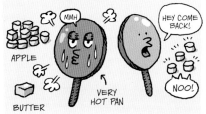

HOW TO MAKE A REAL Quenelle

THE OTHER DAY, I WAS REALLY ANNOYED. I'LL EXPLAIN:

I WANTED TO MAKE QUENELLES. USUALLY, I OPEN A BOX MIX AND THAT'S IT. HOWEVER...

Shoot! It's expired! Gah this sucks! This stuff's expensive! It includes eggs, it's not worth risking it. Gah, into the trash.

12.11.98

BUT THAT WASN'T WHAT ANNOYED ME THE MOST. IT WAS WHEN I DECIDED THAT I WAS GOING TO...

So... Q.U.E.N.E... let's see... click Search CHOOO KAKAO! CHO CHO CHO CHOCOLAT! What the—

NO RECIPES. SOME SONGS BY ANNIE CORDY, SOMETHING ABOUT SOCCER, THE LIFE OF CHRIST...

What is this crap?

ELKA: ELLES, ET ON POUR LISSER AU OURRIS. JÉSUS MANGEAIT ELLES LE LUNDI À LA PISCINE

CLICK

BUT NOTHING ABOUT QUENELLES.

I WAS MAD. AT THE INTERNET, WEB INDEXING, AT PEOPLE.

Yes, could I talk to Sonia, please. Definitely interrupt her, it's urgent. yes Yeah, Sonia? So... I need a recipe for quenelles. Yeah THE recipe? Nah, I don't have a box mix. yeah For? For the good of humanity!

NOT ONLY WAS I GOING TO MAKE QUENELLES, BUT I WAS ALSO GOING TO WRITE THE RECIPE FOR YOU, MY READERS WHO NEED IT. FOR **GASTRONOMY**.

FOR THAT, I WOULD GO STRAIGHT TO THE TOP:

WOOO-HAH!

SONIA EZGULIAN chef from Lyon*

I'm on my way to the store. Water? Got it. Bread flour? Got it. Organic eggs? I'll get some. Butter? Ok. A pike? I'll fish one, BRB Chicken instead? I'll raise one and then be ready. Ok talk soon. You too

TO MAKE QUENELLES FOR SIX (I DON'T HAVE THE PATIENCE TO MAKE A RECIPE FOR THREE, AND I'M HUNGRY), YOU'LL NEED:

1 CUP WATER — 1 1/4 CUPS FLOUR — 3 EGGS — 1/2 STICK BUTTER — 3/4 LB RAW CHICKEN OR PIKE (ALSO RAW)

1 IN A LARGE POT, GENTLY HEAT THE BUTTER AND WATER:

Easy does it

NEXT, DUMP IN THE FLOUR, ALL AT ONCE:

POOF! Easy phile you phake

AS YOU STIR CONSTANTLY OVER VERY LOW HEAT, YOU ARE MAKING A...

PANADE

*SONIA INVENTED COOKING. LYON INVENTED THE QUENELLE. FOR SOME CONTEXT.

The secret is to dry out the panade by stirring it for a long time... yeah, I'm writing it down. You can let it dry overnight as well? Okay.

No, I'm going grocery shopping.

QUACK QUACK

No, that's not a duck.

2 NEXT, INCORPORATE THE EGGS ONE BY ONE INTO THE PANADE:

FIRST HIM, THEN HIM. THEN HIM.

OBVIOUSLY, YOU SHOULD CRACK THEM FIRST, NOT DO EXACTLY HOW IT'S DRAWN. ALSO, EGGS DON'T JUMP; THEY JUST LIE THERE ON THE TABLE. ANYWAY. MIX VERY WELL DURING THIS STEP:

BY HAND — UGH! — OR BY MIXER — BVVV

3 GRIND THE MEAT OR THE FISH, IF NEEDED (YES, AT THIS STAGE, YOU'LL DECIDE YOU'RE NO LONGER HUNGRY, AND THAT'S NORMAL):

SCHL SCHL — FLFL FLFL

OR ASK YOUR BUTCHER OR YOUR FISHMONGER TO DO IT. AFTER ALL, THESE JOBS EXIST FOR A REASON.

4 INCORPORATE THE GROUND MEAT INTO THE PANADE AND STIR AGAIN. YEP. MAKING QUENELLES TAKES MORE THAN JUST SNAPPING YOUR FINGERS:

THE MIXTURE IS NOW WELL-MIXED. THE BATTER IS AS SMOOTH AS A SONG BY MICHAEL BUBLÉ. IT'S COOLED: NOW YOU'RE GOING TO FORM YOUR QUENELLES!

Yeah... still getting groceries...yeah... what? Why I...

SHIIIIT

Ah, no, they were out of box mixes.

Yeah, or else I wouldn't have bothered you.

Good point.

No, that's not a chick.

PEEP PEEP PEEP PEEP

5 TO FORM YOUR QUENELLES, IT TAKES A LITTLE PRACTICE AND A BETTER DRAWING THAN THIS ONE. BUT BASICALLY:

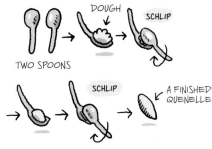

TWO SPOONS — DOUGH — SCHLIP — SCHLIP — A FINISHED QUENELLE

HEY, IT'S FUNNY THAT A QUENELLE IS JUST AS INTERESTING TO DRAW AS AN ANCHOVY (SEE TDTE 1).

6 YOU CAN ALSO FORM THEM BY HAND ON A WELL-FLOURED SURFACE:

BUT... GOOD LUCK. AFTER THAT, YOU COOK YOUR QUENELLES IN SIMMERING WATER (IF IT BOILS, YOU'RE FUCKED):

FLFLFL — (AND NOT "BLOBLOBL")

SIDE PROFILE

When they float to the surface, they're ready. Then you can cook them in tomato sauce or a mushroom cream sauce by putting the sauce in a baking dish, putting the quenelles on top, and sticking everything into the oven for about fifteen minutes at 400°F.

There you have it. Quenelles.

SCRR SCR

GEESH. I GUESS I'LL JUST MAKE MYSELF SOME DAUPHINOISE POTATOES INSTE...WHAT THE FRICK, ARE YOU KIDDING ME?!

EXPIRED.

WHAT'S WRONG WITH THIS FRIDGE?

PEEP

lon.

① FINELY CHOP THE ONION:

BROWN THE MEAT IN A PAN WITH SOME BUTTER AND THE CHOPPED ONION:

TSCHHHHHH   TSCHHH

SEASON EVERYTHING WITH SALT AND PEPPER AND ADD SOME CUMIN TO TASTE (YOU CAN ALSO EXPERIMENT WITH CURRY POWDER OR CORIANDER).

② CUT THE CAULIFLOWER INTO FLORETTES FOR WHATEVER QUANTITY YOU WANT (THIS IS GOING TO REPLACE THE POTATOES IN THE SHEPHERD'S PIE):

BLANCH THEM FOR THREE MINUTES IN A POT OF BOILING SALTED WATER.

FLOPFLOP

③ MAKE A BÉCHAMEL SAUCE (IT'S EASY): LIGHTLY TOAST THREE TABLESPOONS OF FLOUR IN A VERY HOT SAUCEPAN.

NOTHING ELSE?

Yes, just the flour.

...

THEN ADD A KNOB OF BUTTER, AND MIX UNTIL YOU GET A KIND OF PASTE. DON'T LET IT BURN!

④ LITTLE BY LITTLE, ADD THE MILK WHILE MIXING WELL. IT SHOULD MAKE A BÉCHAMEL!

SHHH   FLF   FLF

ADJUST THE QUANTITY AND THICKNESS OF YOUR SAUCE BY ADDING MORE MILK OR FLOUR. SEASON WITH SALT AND GRATED NUTMEG.

⑤ GRATE THE DRY BREAD UNTIL IT FORMS CRUMBS. PREHEAT YOUR OVEN TO 400°F, AND IN A CASSEROLE DISH, ARRANGE YOUR CAULIFLOWER SHEPHERD'S PIE LIKE THIS:

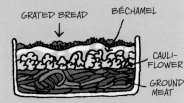

GRATED BREAD   BÉCHAMEL
CAULI-FLOWER
GROUND MEAT

NEXT, COOK FOR... I DON'T QUITE REMEMBER... A GENEROUS FIFTEEN MINUTES?

HERE'S THE FINISHED PRODUCT!

I TASTED AND TESTED THIS, AND IT'S REALLY GOOD, ON MY HONOR!

BUT WHAT ABOUT ME?

THAT SAID, IT WAS MISSING SOMETHING. CAULIFLOWER, CUMIN, BÉCHAMEL, ALL THIS SWEETNESS...

"THINK OF THE ITALIANS," I SAID.

THINK GREMOLATA.

REMEMBER OSSO BUCCO.

⑥ SO THE KILLER PART OF THIS RECIPE IS SOME FINELY MINCED LEMON ZEST MIXED IN WITH THE BREAD:

OKAY, I THOUGHT SO!

THERE YOU GO, BON APPÉTIT!

PARSLEY GARNISH ADDED BY SOME ASSHOLE

Copyright Guillaume Long

leon.

Culinary Tips and Research, Inc.

Tips for the kitchen

Welcome to the headquarters of **C**ulinary **T**ips and **R**esearch, Inc.

A 100% French initiative.

Even though we have some English-speaking readers tonight.

The entire team is here with us to suggest some culinary tips that will simplify your life!

Here, everything has been tested and verified.

Naturally, for the most part, old wives' tales have been rejected.

Hello, Jean-Pierre!

HOLDING A MATCH BETWEEN YOUR TEETH WHEN CHOPPING ONIONS, THAT'S JUST CRAZY!

Haha!

MAKES YOU LOOK LIKE AN ASSHOLE!

The information is updated in real time.

And here is the brain room, where we gather our exclusive, authenticated cooking tips!

The great cooks of the past have been brought back to life!

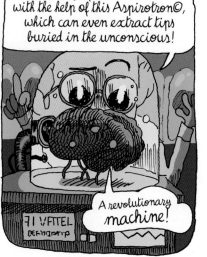

The sorting of this data is done with the help of this Aspirotron©, which can even extract tips buried in the unconscious!

A revolutionary _machine!_

This information (when judged useful, because the unconscious can trick us from time to time, as we all know*) is transported through these tubes...

To the computer room.

*AS WITH FREUD.

And here is where our info sheets (distributed to a number of newspapers and websites) are edited, then printed...

Here it is, our **J.C.N.-9000** at work!

Excellent! Let me show you some of our most famous tips.

Except this one. The world is not ready.

Or this one.

Not this one, either.

Let's see.

Culinary Tips and Research, Inc.

TIP: TO REHEAT COLD PASTA FROM THE NIGHT BEFORE (THE KIND THAT STICKS TOGETHER AND MAKES YOU WANT TO THROW IT IN THE TRASH), JUST ADD BOILING WATER AND WAIT LESS THAN A MINUTE:

RESULT: AFTER YOU DRAIN IT, MIRACLE! HOT PASTA JUST LIKE YESTERDAY'S, MADE WITHOUT HAVING TO USE A FUCKING MICROWAVE.

TIP: TO SUCCESSFULLY MAKE WHIPPED CREAM, THE SECRET IS THE TEMPERATURE. THE CREAM SHOULD COME DIRECTLY FROM THE FRIDGE, AND THE BOWL AND WHISK SHOULD SPEND AT LEAST HALF AN HOUR IN THE FREEZER:

RESULT: A CREAM THAT RISES AS CERTAINLY AS JIM WHITTAKER, WITH PEAKS AS STIFF AS TOM CRUISE. CONSIDER WEARING MITTENS.

TIP: TO SELECT A LIVE LOBSTER OUT OF A TANK (SINCE YOU DON'T DO THIS OFTEN, THIS TIP IS EVEN MORE IMPORTANT), LOOK FOR THE ONE WITH THE LONGEST ANTENNAS:

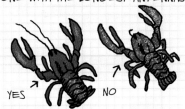

SINCE THESE CRUSTACEANS FREQUENTLY FIGHT, A LOBSTER WITH BIG ANTENNAS IS EITHER THE STRONGEST OR THE MOST RECENT ARRIVAL TO THE TANK. **RESULT:** A DIFFICULT END OF THE MONTH.

TIP: TO KEEP FROM CRYING WHILE CHOPPING AN ONION, ONE EASY SOLUTION: USE A SUPER SHARP KNIFE:

INTERESTINGLY, A DULL KNIFE SMASHES THE ONION, RELEASING MORE OF ITS IRRITATING SUBSTANCE INTO THE AIR **RESULT:** MONEY SAVED ON SWIMMING GOGGLES AND NO MORE RABID RABBIT EYES.

TIP: TO CHOOSE A VERY FRESH FISH, ENSURE THAT THE SCALES ARE FIRMLY ATTACHED, THE GILLS ARE RED, THE EYES ARE PLUMP (CONVEX), THE ABDOMEN IS FIRM, AND THE... UH...ANUS IS CLOSED. IT SHOULD NOT FLOP OVER WHEN YOU HOLD IT BY THE TAIL:

RESULT: AN EXCELLENT FISH THAT DOESN'T UPSET YOUR STOMACH, ONE THAT SYLVESTER THE CAT WOULD KILL FOR. BUYING FILETS INSTEAD? GOOD LUCK.

TIP: DRY BEANS, LIKE LENTILS, BEANS, AND CHICKPEAS, MUST NOT BE SALTED UNTIL TWO-THIRDS THROUGH THEIR COOKING:

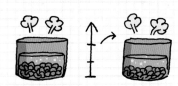

BECAUSE SALTING TOO EARLY HARDENS THEIR SKINS.

RESULT: BIG SAVINGS ON TRIPS TO THE DENTIST.

TIP: WHEN BEATING EGG WHITES, WORK AT ROOM TEMPERATURE. ALSO, THE OLDER THE EGGS, THE BETTER IT WORKS:

RESULT: EGG WHITES AS FIRM AS CHRISTIANO RONALDO'S THIGHS. JUST DON'T USE EGGS THAT ARE TOO OLD.

TIP: FOR A SUCCESSFUL TART CRUST, USE A HIGH GLUTEN FLOUR, BECAUSE THE HIGHER THE GLUTEN, THE EASIER THE DOUGH WILL BE TO ROLL OUT. WHEN YOU LET IT REST, IT WILL FLATTEN RATHER THAN TIGHTENING INTO A BALL.

RESULT: THE CRUST WILL REST BETTER, ROLL OUT MORE EASILY, AND WILL NOT RETRACT IN ITS PAN LIKE A FACELIFT ON VLADIMIR PUTIN.

TIP: TO CONSERVE HALF OF A RIPE AVOCADO WITHOUT ITS FLESH TURNING BLACK, DON'T REMOVE THE PIT:

BUT CAREFUL, IT DOESN'T KEEP INDEFINITELY!

RESULT: AN AVOCADO AS BEAUTIFUL AS ARNO KLARSFELD (A HOT PERSON). GOOD NEWS: THIS ALSO WORKS FOR GUACAMOLE.

Culinary Tips and Research. Inc.

>>TIPS>N>0803>CTR>>
>>VEGE>>99/100>FR>>

TIP: TO KEEP VEGETABLES GREEN AFTER COOKING, KEEP THE COOKING WATER FROM BEING TOO ACIDIC. FOR THAT, ADD BAKING SODA OR A HEAVY DOSE OF SALT (IT SHOULD BE AS SALTY AS THE SEA):

YOU MUST ALSO STOP THE COOKING WITH ICE WATER, AS PROLONGED COOKING WILL DISCOLOR VEGETABLES.
RESULT: GREENER THAN THE GIANT.

>>TIPS>N>3078>CTR>>
>>CRUS>>88/100>FR>>

TIP: TO HAVE A FLAKIER PIE CRUST, ADD A PINCH OF BAKING POWDER.

THIS TECHNIQUE HORRIFIES PURISTS AND CONSERVATIVES, BUT IT ACTUALLY WORKS.

RESULT: A CRUST AS TENDER AND SOFT AS THE CHEST OF MONICA BELLUCCI. I MEAN, WE THINK.

Ah, yes... You have certainly noticed a touch of humor (our most regular asset here at C.T.R.), which is the initiative of Roger D., a colleague who recovered the brain of his brother.

Brain in a pitiful state, that being said.

We need to adjust these settings.

Anyway, let's continue.

>>TIPS>N>8639>CTR>>
>>FING>>96/100>FR>>

TIP: TO KEEP YOUR FINGERS FROM SMELLING LIKE GARLIC AFTER CHOPPING OR MINCING, JUST RUB MOIST HANDS AGAINST ANY KIND OF STAINLESS STEEL:

RESULT: SATISFACTION GUARANTEED AFTER TEN EASY PAYMENTS OF $19.99!

>>TIPS>N>9012>CTR>>
>>LEMO>>65/100>FR>>

TIP: WHEN YOU ONLY WANT TO JUICE A LEMON, MAKE A LITTLE HOLE IN BOTH ENDS AND SQUEEZE:

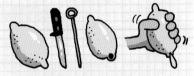

RESULT: NO MORE DRIED LEMON HALVES CLUTTERING YOUR COUNTERTOP (EVEN THOUGH THEY MAKE GREAT ODOR NEUTRALIZERS FOR YOUR FRIDGE).

>>TIPS>N>0039>CTR>>
>>VINE>>96/100>FR>>

TIP: TO MAKE A VINAIGRETTE TASTE AS IF IT'S MADE OF NUT OIL WITHOUT USING NUT OIL (YES, THIS IS A THING), JUST ADD A LITTLE CURRY:

RESULT: A VINAIGRETTE TASTING MORE NUTTY THAN THE REAL THING, AS WELL AS THE JEALOUSY-TINGED ADMIRATION OF ALL YOUR FRIENDS.

>>TIPS>N>2144>CTR>>
>>PAST>>99/100>FR>>

TIP: FOR PASTA THAT DOES NOT STICK TOGETHER, OBSERVE THE RULE OF 1/10/100.

1 LITER OF WATER   10 G OF SALT   100 G OF PASTA

RESULT: TIME TO LEARN THE METRIC SYSTEM.

>>TIPS>N>2146>CTR>>
>>TOMA>>92/100>FR>>

TIP: TO AVOID MAKING A TOMATO DISH (RAGU, RATATOUILLE, OR PASTA SAUCE) THAT IS OVERLY ACIDIC, JUST ADD A SUGAR CUBE DURING COOKING:

RESULT: A BALANCED TASTE, NO MORE SQUINTY CLINT EASTWOOD EYES, AND A HARD BLOW FOR ALL DIABETICS.

>>TIPS>N>9399>CTR>>
>>CANT>>30/100>FR>>

TIP: TO CHOOSE A CANTALOUPE, MAKE SURE IT IS HEAVY, THAT ITS STEM GIVES TO THE TOUCH, AND THAT ITS SMELL IS AGREEABLE BUT NOT TOO STRONG:

NO   YES   NO

BUT IT'S RATHER SUBTLE. AND IT DOESN'T WORK IF FIFTY PEOPLE HAVE PRESSED THE STEM BEFORE YOU.
RESULT: THREE TIMES OUT OF TEN.

>>TIPS>N>4852>CTR>>
>>POTA>>98/100>FR>>

TIP: TO EASILY REMOVE THE SKIN OF BAKED POTATOES, PIERCE THE SKIN PRIOR TO BAKING AND DUNK THEM IN ICED WATER AFTERWARDS:

RESULT: BIG SAVINGS ON ALOE VERA, AND NO MORE SECOND-RATE RACLETTES WITH FRIENDS.

>>TIPS>N>5007>CTR>>
>>TART>>98/100>FR>>

TIP: TO KEEP A TART CRUST FROM GETTING SOGGY FROM A FRESH FRUIT FILLING, DUST IT WITH ALMOND POWDER OR SEMOLINA:

IT WILL ABSORB SOME OF THE JUICE. IT ALSO WORKS WITH RICE, BUT IT'S NOT GOOD.
RESULT: NO MORE TART CRUSTS AS STICKY AS A POISE PAD LEFT ON GRANDMA.

>>TIPS>N>2176>CTR>>
>>PLAS>>78/100>FR>>

TIP: TO KEEP FROM GETTING FRUSTRATED AT THE ~~FUCKING DUMB-ASS~~ ANNOYING ~~AS SHIT~~ PLASTIC WRAP (YOU KNOW, THE ~~FUCKING STUFF~~ THE STUFF THAT STICKS TO YOUR FINGERS), JUST STORE IT IN THE FRIDGE OR THE FREEZE:

IT WILL WRAP UP FOOD AND NOT YOUR HANDS.

RESULT: IT'S COOL.

>>TIPS>N>9534>CTR>>
>>MEAT>>93/100>FR>>

TIP: TO FINISH A PIECE OF MEAT (FILET, ROAST, RIBS, ETC.), YOU SHOULD LET IT REST IN A WARM PLACE, IDEALLY FOR THE LENGTH OF ITS COOKING (BUT NOT AN HOUR, EITHER).

ITS JUICE WILL DIFFUSE INTO THE MEAT INSTEAD OF RUNNING OUT LIKE A INFECTED PIMPLE
RESULT: MEAT AS TENDER AS A CHET BAKER ALBUM.

>>TIPS>N>7352>CTR>>
>>LETT>>99/100>FR>>

TIP: TO REVIVE LIMP LETTUCE, SOAK ITS LEAVES IN A LITTLE WATER OVERNIGHT IN THE FRIDGE:

ONCE HYDRATED, THEY WILL RETURN TO THE BRILLIANCE OF THEIR YOUTH.

RESULT: LETTUCE AS FRESH AS JULIA ROBERTS WHEN FILMING MYSTIC PIZZA.

>>TIPS>N>0495>CTR>>
>>POTA>>82/100>FR>>

TIP: TO KEEP GRATED POTATOES FROM STICKING TO THE PAN, WASH THEM AFTER THEY ARE PEELED, AND DRY THEM WITH A CLEAN TOWEL:

THIS WILL REMOVE SOME OF THEIR STARCH (USED FOR MAKING GLUE, AMONG OTHER THINGS), AND THEY WILL STICK LESS.
RESULT: MAYBE YOU DON'T CARE, BUT IT ALSO WORKS FOR FRIES.

>>TIPS>N>6969>CTR>>
>>TITS>>96/100>FR>>

TIP: FOR A PAIN-FREE WAY TO ENERGIZE YOUR DANCERS' NIPPLES, RUB WITH AN ICE CUBE JUST BEFORE GOING ON STAGE:

THE NIPPLES WILL RISE JUST AS SURELY AS AN AMERICAN FLAG IN A ROLAND EMMERICH FILM.

RESULT: SATISFACTION, ALTHOUGH CAREFUL WITH IMPLANTS, AS THERE MAY BE SOME SURPRISES.

EVEN THOUGH I'VE LIVED FOR SOME TIME IN LYON (IT'S ON MY WIKIPEDIA© PAGE), I DON'T KNOW LYONNAISE CUISINE VERY WELL.

EXCEPT FOR A BOUCHON OR TWO.

IT'S SIMPLE, EVERYDAY FOOD...BUT FOOD THAT YOU SHOULD NOT EAT EVERY DAY.

One of the rare recipes from Lyon that I know is...

Well, it actually comes from Dauphiné.

Dauphinoise potatoes

(LET'S PUT "FOR FOUR PEOPLE")

But for this, in Lyon, no one would say "nay"!

Well, I don't eat it!

Shut up, that was for the rhyme!

Salt and pepper

2.5 pounds of potatoes

Nutmeg

Garlic, 1-2 cloves

4 cups milk

Crème fraîche

Butter

① For dauphinoise potatoes, the kind of potato, of course, is of utmost importance. However, since it's only potatoes, they're easy to find:

RUSSET= for its starchiness (read: fluffiest).

RED-SKINNED= for its color and ability to hold up during the cooking process.

HEIRLOOM FINGERLING= for its delicate flavor.

YUKON GOLD= A cross between a white and a yellow potato, it is velvety and versatile.

② Peel the potatoes and rinse them very briefly:

QUICK!

OK!

With a very sharp knife, cut the potatoes in very thin slices (like, 2-3 mm). It's the longest step:

LET'S BEGIN!

③ You can also cut the potatoes with a mandolin, but since you can also cut your fingers with this tool, take it easy:

After slicing, it is crucial to not rinse the potatoes because that would remove the starch. The starch is what will help the dish thicken and become creamy.

④ In a large pot, bring the milk to a simmer with a peeled clove of garlic. Season with salt, pepper, and nutmeg:

Add the potatoes and gently cook for around ten minutes, stirring often. If you don't, the potatoes will stick together, and you'll have to start all over.

⑤ Preheat your oven to 300°F. Take a casserole dish, and rub it with another peeled garlic clove and some butter:

Next, arrange the potatoes in layers in the dish. You can pour the warmed milk all over with (or not) a little crème fraîche:

⑥ Finally, put your (future) dauphinoise potatoes into the oven for a good hour, or even more. Keep an eye on it, but in general, the longer it cooks the better it is.

Serve your potatoes with a good salad and a bottle of Côte-du-Rhône.

lon.

Mini Tarte MANGO Tatins

"A simple dessert..." "...à la cool."

HOLD ON! PREMADE PIE CRUSTS? THAT'S CRAZY! HOME-MADE IS SO MUCH BETTER. AND SO EASY TO MAKE!

(FOR FOUR PEOPLE)

ORANGES — A MANGO — HONEY — A PREMADE PIE CRUST — GROUND GINGER — FOUR RAMEKINS — PARCHMENT PAPER

① BEFORE DOING ANYTHING, PREHEAT YOUR OVEN TO 400°F. EVEN BEFORE READING WHAT'S NEXT, OKAY? A HOT OVEN IS ALWAYS USEFUL.

NEXT, START ON THE... SYRUP:

JUICE TWO ORANGES:

AND HEAT THE JUICE IN A SAUCEPAN ON MEDIUM. ADD A TABLESPOON OF HONEY AND A TABLESPOON OF GINGER.

AND LET IT COOK UNTIL IT HAS THE CONSISTENCY OF SYRUP, LIKE 5-10 MINUTES.

② DURING THIS TIME, PEEL THE MANGO:

AND CUT IT INTO THIN SLICES:

(THE PIT IS FIBROUS AND FLAT)

I'll cut mine into hearts

AND THEN INTO HALF MOONS OR SOMETHING ELSE PRETTY. EVEN THOUGH IT WILL ALL END UP IN THE TARTES.

③ LINE THE RAMEKINS WITH PARCHMENT PAPER:

AND ARRANGE THE MANGO SLICES IN TWO LAYERS:

AND POUR THE SYRUP FROM STEP ① OVER THE MANGO INTO THE RAMEKINS:

HERE HERE HERE HERE

④ FROM THE PIE CRUST, CUT OUT FOUR DISKS THAT ARE JUST A LITTLE LARGER THAN THE RAMEKINS:

THEN PLACE THEM OVER THE MANGO AND THE SYRUP, TUCKING THE ENDS IN WITH YOUR FINGER OR A KNIFE:

lon.

A FEW YEARS AGO (WHEN CULTURAL PROJECTS RECEIVED A LITTLE MORE GOVERNMENT FUNDING THAN THEY DO TODAY), I WAS INVITED BY THE AQUITAINE REGION FOR A WEEK AS ARTIST-IN-RESIDENCE.

IN CONCLUSION... ANY QUESTIONS?

I THINK IT'S LUNCHTIME!

I GAINED MANY GOOD MEMORIES, AS WELL AS FOUR OR FIVE EXTRA POUNDS, BECAUSE I WAS IN THE CITY OF **PAUILLAC** FOR PART OF THE WEEK.

A SINGLE PIZZERIA IN A CITY OF GASTRONOMIC WONDERS?

PACKED, OF COURSE!

WITH A BUDGET OF 25€ (ABOUT $30) PER MEAL, I BASICALLY HOPPED FROM RESTAURANT TO RESTAURANT

Given the price of the menu, some water, I presume?

(PROJECTING)

(THE APPEARANCE OF AN ARTIST)

SOMETIMES, I DIDN'T NEED TO ADD MUCH TO GIVE MYSELF A MEMORABLE MEAL

NAH, I THINK A GLASS OF 1990 CHAMBOLLE-MUSIGNY WOULD GO WELL WITH THE LEG OF DOE, DON'T YOU AGREE?

A-ah, of course, s-sir.

NEEDS TIPS

(THE APPEARANCE OF A FAMOUS ARTIST)

IN PARTICULAR, I REMEMBER A MIND-BLOWING DISH THAT I MANAGED MORE OR LESS TO RECREATE AT HOME:

CUMIN-MARINATED RACK of LAMB with lentils

FOR A WORTHY REPRODUCTION, YOU'LL NEED:

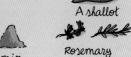

A lemon — A rack of lamb — Lentils — olive oil — honey — salt — pepper — A shallot — Cumin — Rosemary and thyme

① BEGIN BY COOKING THE LENTILS IN BOILING WATER BECAUSE IT ALWAYS TAKES LIKE THREE THOUSAND YEARS. FIGURE OUT THE QUANTITY YOURSELF.

DURING THIS TIME, POSITION YOUR OVEN RACKS BENEATH THE BROILER. THEN, IN A BOWL (FOR A RACK OF LAMB FOR FOUR), MIX:

THE JUICE OF 1/2 LEMON — 2-3 TABLESPOONS OF HONEY — 3-4 TABLESPOONS OF OLIVE OIL — THYME AND ROSEMARY

② SEASON THE RACK OF LAMB WITH SALT AND PEPPER, AND PLACE IN A ROASTING PAN WITH A LITTLE WATER. AROUND TEN MINUTES UNDER THE BROILER, THE BONES WILL BEGIN TO BLACKEN.

CORRECT POSITION: BONES FACING UP

SLATHER THE MEAT WITH THE HONEY MIXTURE, PUT IT BACK UNDER THE BROILER, AND CALMLY LET IT FINISH COOKING.

WHEN IT'S READY, TURN OFF THE OVEN AND LET THE MEAT REST INSIDE (AT THE BOTTOM OF THE OVEN; IF NOT, IT WILL BURN TO A CRISP).

③ WHEN THE LENTILS ARE COOKED, PEEL THE SHALLOT AND CHOP IT FINELY:

BROWN THE SHALLOTS IN A LITTLE OLIVE OIL (IN THE SAUCEPAN THAT YOU USED FOR THE LENTILS, EXCEPT WITHOUT THE LENTILS). SEASON GENEROUSLY WITH CUMIN, THEN STIR IN THE LENTILS, AND SEASON EVERYTHING WITH SALT AND PEPPER!

THE REAL RECIPE HAS TO BE WAY MORE COMPLICATED...

BUT THIS IS PRETTY CLOSE AND COSTS WAY LESS!

lon.

to Happy Hours in Normandy

I'm in the train on my way to...
CAMBREMER

I'm going there for a food festival in order to ①spend two days with a cider producer and ②~~get drunk off my ass~~ understand how it's made, and ③talk to people, like readers like yourself about ④ ~~how to make your own cider~~ for fun.

The whole thing's ~~the fault of~~ thanks to my friend Dominique Hutin (the guy who talks beverages on the radio show "On Va Déguster").

(Dominique loves making jokes over the phone.)

HALLOO, DEES EES HANS GRÜNDTAL, FROM IKEA. WE WEESH TO REQUEST YOUR, AH, TALENT FOR DUH REBRANDING OF OUR CHOCOLATE ALMOND CAKE.

Dominique, I know it's you.

NOO NOT AT ALL! IT'S HANS VARDE!

Jokes that go on for awhile.

HALLOOO? I'M HERE IN SWEDEN, AND YOU'RE BREAKING UP...EES D___ YAS?

Mehh

HAHAHA! JUST KIDDING, IT'S DOMINIQUE!

Really? Hi.

Finally, he suggested this trip, and I said,

I'M DRIVEN TO JUST OUTSIDE OF CAMBREMER, TO THE...

I'LL HAVE AN APPLE JUICE AND THEN I'LL SPLIT.

ACTUALLY, IT WAS NOT LIKE THIS **AT ALL.**

I'M WELCOMED BY THE GRANDOUET FAMILY:

 STÉPHANE

 LUCILE

 ARTHUR

THEIR HOUSE IS DEFINITELY IN THE STYLE OF NORMANDY, BUT IT'S NEW. THE MANOR IS ABOUT 250 YARDS AWAY, IN THE VALLEY.

WHERE I'M GOING

THE MANOR

(THE SHITTY WEATHER DOESN'T CHANGE MUCH.)

GRANDOUET MANOR

Soo...you are here to make some cider?

Heh heh.

The baron of Grandouet will receive you...

You will stay in the manor's north wing.

The room where... hehehe...

LET'S BE CLEAR. I'M COMING HERE WITH A CERTAIN HANDICAP. ALL THAT I KNOW ABOUT CIDER IS:

① ONCE OR TWICE A YEAR, WE DRINK IT IN FRANCE WHILE EATING CRÊPES

I BROUGHT SOME CIDER, I THOUGHT IT'D BE--

HERE.

Oh, awesome, great!

The sweet kind, hopefully?

At least it's less gross than beer!

② FOR A GOOD CIDER, BUY LOÏC RAISON© OR ORGANIC AUCHAN™

SLRRP

FOR $2 BOTTLE, IT'S DEFINITELY GOOD!

SO, RIGHT AWAY, WE BEGIN LEARNING. WE TASTE SOME CIDER THAT HE'S PRODUCED:

 PEAR CIDER FROM I FORGET WHEN

 CIDER FROM 2011 (GOLD MEDAL IN CAMBREMER)

 CIDER FROM I FORGET WHEN (SILVER MEDAL IN PARIS)

 CIDER FROM 2008 (GOLD MEDAL IN PARIS)

I DISCOVER A COMPLEX BEVERAGE WITH NOTES (YES, I SPEAK LIKE A PRO) OF BARK, CITRUS... AND BITTERNESS.

I ALSO DISCOVER THAT THIS BEVERAGE HAS A LOW ABV:

THANKFULLY, LUCILE PREPARED US A LIGHT MEAL:

BASED ON WHAT I UNDERSTAND, THE WORLD OF APPLES IS DIVIDED INTO TWO CATEGORIES:

DWARFING ROOTSTOCKS

A FASTER PRODUCTION OF APPLES (2 TO 3 YEARS), A SHORTER DISTANCE BETWEEN THE TREES, AND A SHORTER LIFE SPAN. IDEAL FOR GETTING STARTED.

FREE-STANDING TREES

A SLOWER PRODUCTION OF APPLES (8 TO 10 YEARS), A TREE THAT CAN LIVE UP TO 100 YEARS, AND CAN LIVE ON A SOIL WEAKER IN NUTRIENTS DUE TO THE DEPTH OF ITS ROOTS.

STÉPHANE SHOWS ME HIS PROPERTY: 70 ACRES OF TREES FOR AN ANNUAL PRODUCTION OF 70,000 BOTTLES OF CIDER.

35 pounds of apples makes 2.5 gallons of cider or a quart of calvados (apple brandy).

The apples for cider aren't for eating. Too much bitterness, not enough acidity.

Blech! What's this shit?

IN NORMANDY, THERE ARE 400 DIFFERENT VARIETIES! THE APPLES AT THE GRANDOUET MANOR THAT STÉPHANE NAMES FROM MEMORY ARE:

la NOËL DES CHAMPS

la CALARD

la FREQUIN ROUGE

la SAINT-MARTIN

Okay, I'm going to explain the cider-making process. It could be a little difficult to capture, but you're taking notes?

Uh 'kay goahead.

What do you mean, difficult?

Depends on your TALENT.

'KAY.

This is nuts! ASHMEAD'S KERNEL, BROWN SNOUT, COX'S ORANGE PIPPEN, FOXWHELP!

The readers are never going to believe these names!

GUIDE TO CIDER APPLES spcc...

Also, I never would have thought apples were so boring to draw.

① <u>harvesting</u> (the month of October)

It's done with the help of a vibrating harvester machine:

Then, the apples are sucked up by a kind of apple vacuum:

I don't really note how to draw it, but basically it groups the apples as well as a border collie herds sheep.

Next, they are collected by a sweeper. (Carefully, because it bruises the apples.)

The last ones are gathered by hand.

Example of a sweeper from Normandy

② <u>cider-making</u>

The apples are washed and sorted by hand until December.

Next, they are sent through the grinder. Out of this comes the apple must (the juice, seeds, and skins). The rest is fed to animals (the pomace).

Finally, the must passes through a press, which extracts the apple juice:

FFLRFRSHTFRHSH

(Not sure if it actually comes out here.)

I actually understood how the press works. It's a large membrane that expands a dozen times in a kind of giant cheese grater:

MFF

SPLRT

MUST

APPLE JUICE

③ fermentation

The apple juice is first exposed to the air for 15 days; then, it is transferred to closed tanks in a cellar at 11°C (51.8°F).

Then you have what we call the... excuse me...defecation. The pectin and other impurities rise to the surface forming what's known as a brown hat or cap. We add some enzymes and calcium, which allows us to obtain a clear juice.

It's important to obtain a good hat, like you see here. It should be between four and six inches thick.

The feathers are just for show.

Next, bubbles begin to form in the juice. Through cracks in the brown hat, you can see some rising to the surface. This is fermentation: what you lose in sugar, you gain in alcohol.

Finally, the cider (not yet carbonated) is siphoned into barrels in a process called "soutirage." Yeast (1.5 g for 100 L) is added in relationship to how much the density of the produce has decreased.

SEMI-SWEET, 3% (2-3 MONTHS OF FERMENTATION)

SEMI-DRY, 4.5% (3-4 MONTHS OF FERMENTATION)

DRY CIDER, 5.5% (5 MONTHS OF FERMENTATION)

The cider that's distilled for calvados is fermented for a year and reaches 7% alcohol.

C'MON GIRLS, LET'S CARBONATE THIS THING.

Soutirage yeast

④ bottling

The cider is bottled by this (completely undrawable) machine that you see behind me... Do you want me to keep talking so that you don't have to draw it, or should I pause for a moment?

Don't tell me that you're playing with my grandfather's model press while I...

N-no, don't worry, I have it all written down in my head!

I um...

You're going to love it!

Grandval's cider production takes place in this picturesque setting. The Grandouet Manor is on the left, and the little house that serves as the store and Lucile's office (adjoining the pond) is on the right. In the back, you can see some out-buildings for storing material and barrels.

AT LUNCHTIME, I EAT WITH STÉPHANE AND LUCILE.

Wow, this lamb is really good!

Hm?

No, that's veal from our farm!

WHAAT? N...NOT THE LITTLE CALF FROM THIS MORNING!

Definitely not! Actually, you are mistaking it for lamb because the meat is brown...that means that the calf has run free. White veal is only possible if a calf has been fed a bunch of drugs and hormones.

AFTERWARDS, WE EAT AN APPLE TART. IT MOVES ME LESS THAN THE BLOW ABOUT THE CALF, BUT IT'S ALSO VERY GOOD.

IN THE AFTERNOON, STÉPHANE TAKES ME TO THE FOOD FESTIVAL BECAUSE I'M PART OF THE PANEL THAT WILL DETERMINE THE BEST A.O.C. CALVADOS OF THE YEAR.

It's crazy. I don't even know how to taste wine. Drinking calva is going to kill me!

So first of all, if you don't want to get yourself killed, throw out your gum before arriving. And second, call it Calvados, not calva.

Stéphane? Yeah?

You just wrote a whole frame for my comic.

THE COMPETITION TAKES PLACE IN A COMMUNITY HALL IN CAMBREMER, AND I'M SENTENCED TO TASTE A.O.C. CALVADOSES, AGED FOUR TO SEVEN YEARS:

UNMARKED BOTTLES

3 GLASSES

A SPITTOON

NOTE PAPER

ACROSS FROM ME (WE'RE ORGANIZED IN TABLES OF FOUR) THERE'S A GUY WHO SEEMS TO KNOW EVERYTHING...

That's funny! These look like vials of pee!

Hilarious. Let's begin.

'Kaysure.

THE COMPETITION QUICKLY BECOMES A BLUR. WE HAVE TO RANK ALL THE SAMPLES BY AROMA (6 POINTS), FIRST IMPRESSION (7 POINTS), THE FINISH (7 POINTS), AND ANY DEFAULTS IN APPEARANCE (REMOVE 1 TO 5 POINTS).

They all have the super strong, burning taste of calva.

3 POINTS. THIS ONE'S NOT GREAT.

DITTO!

UGH, AWFUL!

BAD CALVA

DOS.

EVEN THOUGH I'VE DONE MY BEST TO SPIT AND EAT ALL THE BREAD AND ANDOUILLE DE VIRE AT THE END OF THE ROOM, MY MOUTH IS ON FIRE AFTER SIX SAMPLES.

AROMA, 4 POINTS?

I'LL GIVE IT FIVE.

5? NO, IT'S DEFINITELY WORSE THAN SAMPLE 512!

WHAHEVAH YOO SAY!

AFTER THIRTEEN SAMPLES, THE MUSTACHED GUY ACROSS FROM ME STILL HASN'T SPIT OUT ANYTHING:

IN THE END, I LEAVE THE COMPETITION STUFFED WITH SAUSAGE AND COMPLETELY WASTED. IT'S 5 P.M..

STÉPHANE, AFTER A SHOWER AND SHAVE.

IN THE EVENING, WE'RE INVITED WITH A BUNCH OF PEOPLE FROM THE FESTIVAL FOR THE INAUGURAL MEAL.

the Sense Manor

The ideal location for your uppity soirées.

WE SIP SOME CALVADOS COCKTAILS, WE GET A LITTLE BORED, WE TALK SOME...

(OUR ACTUAL CONVERSATION)

ÉRIC ROUX, FORMER CULINARY TV PERSONALITY

AND SUDDENLY, IT HIT ME. I HAD COMPLETELY FORGOTTEN WE WERE SUPPOSED TO MEET UP WITH HIM THIS EVENING, BUT HE IS THERE:

BLAZER

PAJAMA TOP

ROLLED-UP PANTS

(ONE DAY, I'LL WRITE A BOOK ON DOMINIQUE'S CLOTHING STYLE.)

WICKER SANDALS

NO SOCKS

BUT THE JOY WAS SHORT-LIVED, BECAUSE BEHIND DOMINIQUE, SOMEONE APPEARED LIKE A DEVIOUS SHADOW...

WE GET ALONG WELL WITH OPHÉLIE. THAT'S NOT THE PROBLEM. BUT ON THE SUBJECT OF ALCOHOL, SHE ALWAYS HAS TO HAVE THE FINAL WORD.

HEYY, HOW ARE YOU, HON?

SO, YOU KNOW CIDER, TOO? HEH HEH!

HAVE YOU FIGURED OUT THE DIFFERENCE YET BETWEEN A RED AND A WHITE?

FORGIVE ME, I DIDN'T COME TO THE CALVADOS TASTING PANEL BECAUSE I WAS BEING INTERVIEWED BY FRANCE 3, HEHEHEHEHE!

HEY, DO YOU EVEN KNOW WHAT'S IN YOUR GLASS?

HEHEHE

OPHÉLIE NEIMAN AKA *miss Glou Glou**

*WINE JOURNALIST

It's good. I've learned a lot!

Yeah? Like what?

Well, tho... I already know that. Anything else?

yada yada yada

EVENING HIGHLIGHTS

Norman beef tenderloin with Pommeau sauce, potatoes, and mushrooms

It's um... not bad, uh... but not...

slrpp

It's fine.

"'

Dominique and Stéphane tactfully taste Swedish cider.

Hehe

Z

Ophélie got her picture taken behind a guest who fell asleep at his table.

The starry sky.

Day 2

I TOOK AN ICE-COLD SHOWER BECAUSE THERE WAS NO HOT WATER, AND I'M EATING A MEDIOCRE BREAKFAST WITH SOME WEAK DRIP COFFEE. THANK GOODNESS I WENT OUT OF MY WAY TO SIT ALONE, BECAUSE I'M NOT AT ALL A MORNING PERSON AND DON'T WANT TO TA'...

I wake up in a room fit for Mary Poppins in the middle of nowhere.

AFTER BREAKFAST, I HEAD TO CAMBREMER'S AOC/AOP FESTIVAL WITH STÉPHANE.

Last night was fun, Ophélie seems nic... — NO.

Oh, you thi... — SHH.

(My other half is betraying me.)

Didja sleep well?

grmbl

Delphinius

I took such a hot shower, it was great! I had the "Queen of the Woods" room, what about you?

This seat taken? — Yes.

Thanks!

I stayed in the shower for like 3 hours, not so good for the environment, huh?

Hehe!

Go away.

Ohhh, somebody's grumpy this morning!

I LINGER AMONG THE LOCAL PRODUCERS WHILE WAITING FOR THE AWARDS CEREMONY FOR THE BEST CIDERS OF 2013...

NOWAY, FOURME DE MONTBRISON!

I'M STÉPHANOIS!

Go for it!

↑ LIVED FOR 10 YEARS IN ST.-ÉTIENNE

REBLOCHON CHEESE!

THAT'S FROM MY REGION!

Help yourself!

NOOO, GRUYÈRE, TOO!

DID YOU KNOW I'M SWISS?

Want a piece?

← WAS BORN IN SWITZERLAND

← LIVED FOR 17 YEARS IN HAUTE-SAVOIE

SPENT THREE DAYS IN MADRID →

PARMA HAM!

PERO...YO SOY ITALIANO!

Che stronzo!

MEANING...

Gah, O...Ophélie, I made friends with all the producers, and my stomach can't take it anymore.

Haha, cute.

Do you have any meds?

May. be.

I thought your dad was a doctor?

What if he isn't?

C'mon, it's for my story!

Oh, for real?

Of course! Cough up the Prilosec©!

LATE MORNING, STÉPHANE WINS A BUNCH OF MEDALS FOR HIS CIDER, HIS LIFE, HIS WORK

...medals that touch us both deeply, Stéphane and I. I thoroughly enjoyed working with his gra...apples, and I look forward to an even better cider next year. Notably, I anticipate ...oving upon th... ...as well as the

No flash, please.

AROUND 6 P.M., OPHÉLIE, DOMINIQUE, AND I ~~GET OUT OF THIS PLACE~~ LEAVE THIS LITTLE TOWN TO MEET UP WITH THE TEAM OF "ON VA DÉGUSTER"*, WHO IS RECORDING A SHOW LIVE FROM COUTANCES FOR THEIR WEEK-LONG FESTIVAL, "JAZZ UNDER THE APPLE TREES."

SAYING GOODBYE TO THE GRANDVAL FAMILY IS RATHER HARROWING:

It was great having you with us. Here's some cider so that you'll think of us...come back whenever you'd like, okay?

Okay?

Can't I just leave already?

I hope that he knows we're just being polite.

We'll be able to get back to work.

DOMINIQUE HAS AN ANCIENT PEUGEOT 309, BUT WE MAKE IT TO COUTANCES IN AN HOUR AND FIFTEEN RATHER THAN IN AN HOUR FIFTY-FOUR BECAUSE DOMINIQUE DRIVES FAST. AND POETICALLY.

I put on my grandma's glasses to drive, but now I'm going to wear them for your entire story. They make me look awesome and I know how much you hate drawing eyes...

ready to go?

Someone's feeling bitchy!

hehe

You coming? Dom's waiting.

This is a very badly drawn Peugeot 309.

Hey, have you read *The World According to Garp*? Because you don't have a gear shifter anymore, Dom.

What? What happens in *The World According to Garp*? Shit, Dom, you just... blew a stop sign back there

Dude, I'm free... Signs are for those who choose to stop! I work for France Inter, dude! Radio waits for nobody!

Even though we're recording tomorrow.

IN THE EVENING, I SLEEP SAFE AND SOUND AT COUTANCES IN A HOTEL ACROSS FROM A CATHEDRAL.

My word.

What history!

EXCEPT THAT EARLIER, I HAD EXPERIENCED ONE OF THE CULINARY MOMENTS OF MY LIFE

Suspense!

hehehe...

Okay. Let's go back three hours, when we arrived at Blainville-sur-Mer...

We're not going to Coutances anymore? Where are we? This is the middle of nowhere!

Haha surprise!

Blainville, dude.

We'll wait for the team from France Inter, and we'll have dinner here!

Where's here?

Hahaha!

?

Here, there is a shitty little restaurant on the beach called...

LA CALE

(the beach, Blainville-sur-Mer)

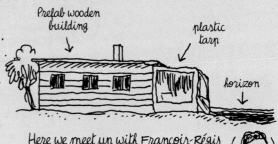

Prefab wooden building

plastic tarp

horizon

Here we meet up with François-Régis

Elvira ( ), Michèle ( )

and Léa ( ), but I'm not going to draw everyone each time.

La Cale

It gets shut down by the health inspector each year, but I love this place!

Let's go in?

Odor of cheap grease

Suspicious-looking sausages

Uncleared tables

Pieces of fat and lettuce

Laminated menu typed on Microsoft Word

Drunk owner

JUST TO LET YOU KNOW, I DON'T SET THE TABLE.

APPARENTLY, ALL PEOPLE FROM NORMANDY HAVE MESSY HAIR.

THE MENU DOESN'T LOOK PROMISING. THERE'S SAUSAGE AND FRIES FOR 8.50€, MUSSELS AND FRIES FOR 11.50€, AND WHELKS WITH MAYONNAISE FOR 6€. BUT DOMINIQUE KNOWS THIS PLACE WELL AND ANNOUNCES:

We'll have the lobster for 25€. With fries and whatever shitty red wine you have because there's nothing* on the menu.

This is going to be good.

What's with the sunglasses, Dominique?

Those awful glasses

It's for my character; I'll explain.

(*Dominique's an enologist.)

WHEN THE OWNER SEES THAT EVERYONE IS ORDERING THE LOBSTER AND THAT HE'S GOING TO TURN HIS BIGGEST PROFIT OF THE YEAR, HE GOES CRAZY:

OKAY, PEOPLE. IF YOU'RE GOING TO ORDER THE LOBSTER, YOU HAVE TO TRY THE WHELKS.

I'LL GO DESALT SOME.

HE GRABS LÉA BY THE ARM:

AND YOU, LITTLE SHRIMP, ARE COMING WITH ME TO HELP!

TO FULLY UNDERSTAND THE STAKES OF THE SCENE, HERE'S A REAL-LIFE PORTRAIT OF LÉA:

THE GAZE OF A FAWN, BLONDE HAIR. LÉA, THE IMAGE OF PURITY.

AND THERE, WE ALL WATCH AS LÉA AND THE OWNER GET INTO A JEEP AND HEAD TOWARD THE HORIZON TO DESALT WHELKS. THE TAILLIGHTS ON THE JEEP GET SMALLER AND SMALLER... AND THEN DISAPPEAR ALTOGETHER.

DOMINIQUE HUTIN, FROM NORMANDY

FRANÇOIS-RÉGIS GAUDRY, CULINARY JOURNALIST

OPHÉLIE NEIMAN, OPTIMIST

MICHÈLE BILLOUD, REALIST

ELVIRA MASSON, HUNGRY

LÉA RETURNS WITHOUT A SCRATCH:

While waiting for the shellfish, I talk with Michèle, who has worked at France Inter for a little while.

THEN, WE ARE SERVED

① The Whelks

I LOVE WHELKS. THESE ARE NO EXCEPTION. THEY'RE MAYBE EVEN BETTER: ABSOLUTELY PERFECT. THEIR FLESH IS DELICATELY SPICY, FIRM, AND TO DIE FOR... YOU COULDN'T GET ANY FRESHER. TO TOP IT OFF WAS THE MAYO WHICH SEEMED HOUSE-MADE. AT ANY RATE, IT WAS GREAT.

AND AT 6€ FOR A BOWL OF TWENTY, THERE WAS NO CONTEST.

ELVIRA AND I WERE OVERLY POLITE:

THE OWNER THEN BRINGS OUT
FOR EACH PERSON:

a lobster
cracker

an apron

a lobster fork

AND HE BRINGS OUT THE LOBSTERS, CAUGHT THAT MORNING.

GIVE THIS A TRY!

ooh

II The lobster

I WON'T MINCE WORDS: IT WAS INCREDIBLE.
I'VE ONLY EATEN LOBSTER THREE OR FOUR
TIMES IN MY LIFE, BUT THIS ONE BEAT ALL.

THE FLESH WAS SALTY, FIRM,
AND DENSE; THE TASTE
WAS DIVINE, AND EACH
LOBSTER WAS BIGGER
THAN ITS PLATE.

WITHOUT GARNISHES, JUST AS
THEY WERE. I EVEN FOR-
GOT ABOUT THE
MAYONNAISE.

25 EUROS. WHAT A STEAL. INCREDIBLE.

THE FRIES WERE ALSO HOUSE
MADE, CUT ROUGHLY
WITH A KNIFE:

THE BEST
JOYS ARE THIS
SIMPLE.

HOW DID YOU
MAKE THE
BROTH?

GAH, WELL,
WE BOILED
THE LOBSTER
FOR FIFTEEN
MINUTES IN
SALTED
WATER

THAT'S
IT?

YES.

INCREDIBLE.

I'LL SAY IT
AGAIN: SO, SO
GOOD!©

LOBSTER IS
PURE PLEASURE.

OPHÉLIE EXPERIENCES...A SORT OF
CULINARY ORGASM:

AGH!
MMM!
SO
GOOD!
MMM!
MMMM!

LÉA'S SUDDENLY THE OWNER'S BEST FRIEND:

SHE TELLS ME THAT IT'S THE FIRST TIME SHE'S EVER HAD LOBSTER. SHE'S THRILLED.

I'M IN HEAVEN. THE PLACE IS CHEERFUL, SIMPLE, AND UNPRETENTIOUS. SOME PEOPLE ARE PLAYING COUNTRY JAZZ IN A CORNER. EVERYONE'S TALKING AT ONCE, GESTURING WIDELY, AND GOING BACK AND FORTH BETWEEN THE BEACH AND THE RESTAURANT.

(*END OF SUSPENSE)

IT'S EXACTLY WHAT I LOVE WHEN I GO ELSEWHERE TO EAT: BEING DISCONCERTED. THE EXPERIENCE OF A 25€ LOBSTER IN THE MIDDLE OF NOWHERE (SIMPLY AND PERFECTLY COOKED) WILL STAY WITH ME LONGER THAN A LOBSTER DECORATED WITH PARSLEY AND BURIED IN THE 180€ MENU AT, SAY, CHEF PAUL BOCUSE. LIFE IS LIKE THAT.

AS FOR DOMINIQUE...

MAYBE IT WAS BECAUSE WE WERE WITH FRANCE INTER. MAYBE IT WAS REAL GENEROSITY.

Day ③

WHEN I ARRIVE AT THE RECORDING, THE BROADCAST IS BASICALLY FINISHED. I MAKE IT JUST IN TIME TO HEAR ELIVRA MAKE A HUGE MISTAKE:

THANK YOU TO EVERYONE, AND LONG LIVE LOBSTERS FROM BRITTANY!

Oooh! Ooooh! Oooohoh!

NORMANDY! HEHE!

WE'RE GOING TO GET OURSELVES KILLED!

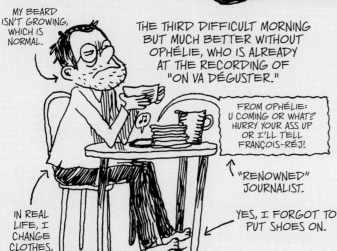

THE THIRD DIFFICULT MORNING BUT MUCH BETTER WITHOUT OPHÉLIE, WHO IS ALREADY AT THE RECORDING OF "ON VA DÉGUSTER."

MY BEARD ISN'T GROWING, WHICH IS NORMAL.

FROM OPHÉLIE: U COMING OR WHAT? HURRY YOUR ASS UP OR I'LL TELL FRANÇOIS-RÉJ!

"RENOWNED" JOURNALIST.

IN REAL LIFE, I CHANGE CLOTHES, 'KAY?

YES, I FORGOT TO PUT SHOES ON.

I SEE SOMEBODY WASN'T UP IN TIME.

HUH? YEAH I--

I DIDN'T SEE YOU HERE.

WELL, BUY SOME EYES.

WHAT WAS THE SHOW ABOUT?

LOBSTER.

WHAT ELSE?

UMM... OTHER STUFF! GAH... DON'T TELL ANYONE, 'KAY?

MMHM.

AFTERWARDS, THE WHOLE TEAM HAS LUNCH WITH SOME OFFICIALS FROM THE MAYOR'S OFFICE. WE'RE SERVED LOCAL OYSTERS AND WHELKS:

NO DIGNITY.

Yaaas! MMMM SLURP BURP

OFFICIAL FROM THE MAYOR'S OFFICE

I ATE AROUND 12,564 OF THEM WHEN IT WAS SUPPOSED TO BE AN APPETIZER. BUT I LOVE OYSTERS, AND WHEN THEY'RE FRESH FROM THE SEA, IT'S JUST HEAVEN:

Fresh!

The man your man could smell like.

OLD SPICE!

AND YOU...WHO ARE **YOU?**

WHA? UM... AN ASSISTANT.

LOOKS LIKE YOU LIKE OYSTERS!

A LITTLE.

MH.

WHAT DO YOU DO FOR THE BROADCASTS?

THINGS. I BOUGHT THE LOBSTER.

FOR EXAMPLE.

OH? WHERE?

FROM A GUY.

ANOTHER OFFICIAL FROM THE MAYOR'S OFFICE

AROUND **1 P.M.**, WE HEAD TO THE FARM OF...

SPECIALTY SHEEP FARMER AND PRODUCER OF HERITAGE VEGETABLES

I made some lamb, mussels, fries, and some dauphinoise potatoes. Is that okay?

HIS GREENHOUSES AND HIS SHEEP ARE HIDDEN IN A FOREST NEXT TO SOME SALT MEADOWS, WHERE THE SHEEP GRAZE.

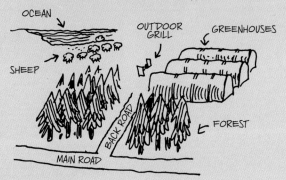

BY THE WAY HE TALKS ABOUT HIS WORK, YOU CAN TELL RIGHT AWAY THAT GÉRARD LOVES HIS SHEEP. IN THE SUMMER, HE USES GREENHOUSES FOR HIS VEGETABLES (INCLUDING TOMATOES THAT ARE OUT OF THIS WORLD). BUT HE ADMITS THAT HE MOST LOVES HIS SHEEP ON A GRILL!

AS SOON AS WE ARRIVE, SOMETHING UNEXPECTED HAPPENS:

Ooh...the poor, hurt sheep... What happened?

He was attacked by a dog.

Ohhh!

I've been bringing out the hypnotist each week to help him out.

Oooh...

Along with the veterinarian, of course.

I hope we're not going to eat this thing.

groo

BEHHH!!

NO EMOTION

JUNK

LEG OF LAMB

SAUSAGES

TSHHHH

SCHLSCHHH

I no longer have the A.O.C. certification because it pissed me off that people behind desks got to decide when I brought in my sheep at night. My lamb is excellent regardless.

DOMINIQUE KNOWS THIS PLACE WELL. FOR THE OCCASION, HE HAS BROUGHT A

CHÂTEAU CARBONNIEUX 1922.

THIS COULD BE REALLY, REALLY INTERESTING.*

DUDE! WHAT'S WITH THE SUNGLASSES?

WE'LL TALK ABOUT IT LATER, 'KAY?

HHHHH!!!

CALM DOWN, OPHÉLIE.

*IN THE ENOLOGY WORLD, "INTERESTING" MEANS THAT IT'S NOT NECESSARILY GOOD BUT IS INSTEAD COMPLETELY AMAZING. LIKE IMPROV JAZZ.

THE MEAL IS MEMORABLE. I THINK THAT I WILL REMEMBER THIS MOMENT FOR YEARS...

① *We begin with the mussels.*

TO GIVE YOU A VAGUE IDEA OF THEIR TASTE, LET'S JUST SAY THAT THEY ARE THE BEST MUSSELS I'VE EATEN IN MY LIFE. AND YES, I ALREADY WENT ON ABOUT THE LOBSTER, BUT IT'S NOT MY FAULT THAT I'VE EATEN SO WELL THESE FEW DAYS.

SO HOW DO YOU COAX OUT SUCH A PURE TASTE FROM THESE MUSSELS? BY WHAT MIRACLE? WHAT OINTMENT? WHAT SECRET BROTH?

MMM! SLURP! GULP! GARP!

JUST WATER, REALLY.

IMPOSSIBLE!

LIKE THE LOBSTER? NAHH...

OH YES!

IT'S SO, SO GOOD©!

② *We continue with the fries and the salad.*

I HAVE A PRETTY INTERESTING DISCUSSION WITH OPHÉLIE EVEN THOUGH SHE WAS BASICALLY TALKING NONSENSE:

I'd say that a bottle of white from 1922 is more impressive than a mussel from the sea. Think of the years of work from the viticulteurs, yeah, sorry not sorry!

Fuck you, this is the pure taste of a mussel! From nature directly to your taste buds!

Meh.

No manipulation, anything!

You're crazy!

The labor matters more to me.

Oh yeah? What about the labor of Chinese children that makes the sneakers that you wear? Does that matter to you, huh, you

THE CONVERSATION BREAKS DOWN FROM HERE.

The secret to a good fry is to cook it twice and let it cool in between.

That, and Crisco.

Just kidding! That's no dud, spud!

OKAY NO...

LISTEN, SON... YOU SHOULD WORK ON USING LESS TEXT.

IT'S A COMIC, NOT A FUCKIN' BOOK.

JOANN SFAR ALREADY GIVES US PAGES OF WRITING.

THIS DOESN'T WORK AT ALL.

(MR. PUBLISHER)

I DUNNO, DRAW SOME FRAMES, INCLUDE STAGE DIRECTIONS OR SOME VANISHING POINTS, BUT SHIT, DRAW ME A COMIC!

MAKE SURE IT SELLS.

THEN, WE FEAST UPON HIS LAMB.

LET'S RAISE A GLASS TO MY PUBLISHER!

YOU AND YOUR MUSSELS C[A] FUCK OF[F]

THE SUN SHONE IN THE SKY AS IN OUR HEARTS.

SO, SO GOO[D]

POOR BOY.

IS THIS SAUSAGE FROM BRITTANY?

HEHE!

ITS PREPARATION WAS SIMPLE, BUT THE MEAT WAS WITHOUT COMPARISON.

THERE WERE SAUSAGES AND THE LEG OF LAMB, ACCOMPANIED BY THE DAUPHINOISE POTATOES IN HONOR OF A CERTAIN GUEST.

PURE HAPPINESS.

AFTER THE MEAL, WE FAN OUT AROUND THE FARM.

I'M PONY CLUB-TRAINED.

GO AHEAD, TAKE A PICTURE.

OPHÉLIE RODE A HORSE.

FRANÇOIS-RÉGIS THOROUGHLY ENJOYED THE DOGS.

Oh, hehehehe, who's a good dog, huh? Heyyy Guillaume, don't draw this in your journal, okay?

HE HE

Of course not!

I'll respect your privacy.

ELVIRA WANDERED OFF TO THE SALT MEADOWS.

DOMINIQUE AND I CONTINUE TO DRINK.

Here, I have some calva that doesn't suck.

dos

Pop it open!

'kay!

120

I ~~GET THE HECK OUT~~ LEAVE NORMANDY THE NEXT DAY. THE EVENING BEFORE, I STAY AT DOMINIQUE'S HOUSE.

THIS IS NICE. DO YOU HAVE WIFI?

NO, I WORK WITH FRANCE INTER BY TELEX.

OH YEAH, REALLY!

?

I MEET HIS WIFE:

OH SORRY, I'M JUST GETTING BACK FROM A SWIM

WHO ARE THESE CRAZY PEOPLE?

WHAAT? YOU MUST BE FREEZING!

NO, I SWIM ALL THE TIME, EVEN IN THE WINTER!

DO YOU HAVE A CONDITION WHERE YOU--

HAHA! NO, I JUST LOVE IT!

MAYBE IT'S ME WHO'S CRAZY.

NOOO...

THE COLDEST I EVER WENT SWIMMING WAS 45 DEGREES!

SINCE WE WEREN'T TOO HUNGRY AND MOSTLY FUCKED UP, DOMINIQUE SUGGESTS BEFORE GOING TO BED:

A BEER FOR YOU WHO HATES BEER! HAHA!

A 2001 CANTILLON, DUDE!

FROM THE LAMBIC FAMILY!

(SINCE I WROTE A STORY ON THE FACT THAT I HATE BEER*, HOP LOVERS EVERYWHERE WANT ME TO DRINK THIS BEVERAGE AND SECRETLY THINK THAT I WILL CHANGE MY MIND.)

*READ TO DRINK AND TO EAT VOLUME 2.

SO?

IT... IT'S...

IT'S?

CRAP, WHAT'S THE WORD?

IT'S INTERESTING!

THIS COULD BE USEFUL IN GUANTANAMO.

HHHA!

AND DISGUSTING.

SCRRR

SEE! YOU LIKE BEER!

JUST GOOD BEER.

I SLEEP IN THE BED OF HIS SON, BOB.*

YOU OKAY?

YEP.

WE DON'T HAVE A LIGHT BECAUSE BOB PRETENDED TO BE TARZAN

IT'S FINE.

WE MADE THIS CAVE WITH SHOWER CURTAINS.

NO WORRIES, IT'S COOL.

IT'S LIKE THAT AT DOMINIQUE'S: EVERY WHICH WAY.

*NAME CHANGED

 **Day ④**

WE ARE DRIVING AT BREAKNECK SPEED ACROSS A GRANDIOSE COUNTRYSIDE OF MOORS, ROCKS THAT LOOK LIKE THEY'VE BEEN LASER-CUT, AND WHITE-SAND BEACHES. DOMINIQUE HAS MADE US A RESERVATION FOR A RESTAURANT AN HOUR AND FIFTEEN MINUTES FROM HIS HOUSE, AND WE HAVE 45 MINUTES TO GET THERE.

(EARLIER)

(HALLO? HANS, RESERVATION FOR TWO, PLEESE.)

UNDER DUH NAME OF HANS GRÜNDTAL, YAS. *(They know me around here. I have to be clever.)*

TYPICAL DOMINIQUE!

OH LORD!*

HAVE FUN. I'M GOING FOR A SWIM.

*I IMAGINE SHE'S BEEN SAYING THIS FOR TEN YEARS!

WE MAKE IT TO...

La malle aux épices

(71 RUE DE L'ÉGLISE, 50440 AUDERVILLE)

Restaurant

Ocean

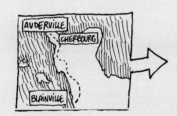

DOMINIQUE LOVES THIS RESTAURANT. IT MAKES SENSE: YOU EAT WELL FOR $25 WITHOUT DRINKS. AND THE TRIP THERE IS SO BEAUTIFUL...

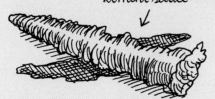

Tempura blue ling fish, kimchi sauce

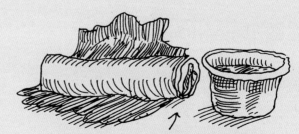

Egg roll with vegetables and feta, honey and rosemary dipping sauce

In our glasses, a Charles Pain Chinon from 2012

IT'S GOOD. WE'LL TAKE IT.

INTERESTING?

SLRRP. NO! THIS ONE'S GOOD.

Shrimp, bamboo, and mushroom sauté ↓

Mouline of sumac, Madagascar pepper, mashed potatoes, and wasabi ↑

Salad of asparagus, tomatoes, and beef hearts with a Thai vinaigrette ↓

Carpaccio of Saint-Jacques scallops and chervil root ↓

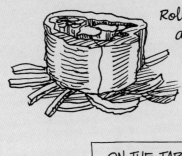

Roll of salmon, yuzu, and green mango ↓

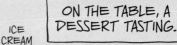

For dessert, we head out onto the deck to enjoy the sun.

ON THE TABLE, A DESSERT TASTING.

ICE CREAM

SUMKINDA PASTRY

MANGO SKEWER

SUMKINDA ROLL

SUMKINDA EGG ROLL

YUZU CRÈME ANGLAISE

CRÈME BRÛLÉE

AND THIS IS HOW MY JOURNEY TO NORMANDY ENDS: IN A FRENZY AND WITH A TRAFFIC JAM IN THE CITY.

DOMINIQUE RUNS AFTER ME TO GIVE ME STÉPHANE'S CIDER.

WHEN YOU FINISH YOUR BEST TRIPS IN A HURRY, YOU CAN AVOID THINKING ABOUT WHAT YOU'VE LEFT BEHIND.

lon.

Pépé Roni's Good Advice: Nuns' Farts   Nº 902

Don't confuse "Nuns' Farts"

PFFARRROUUIT!

and "Nun Departs"

PATISSERIES

BECAUSE ANYONE CAN MAKE MISTAKES!

Nuns' Farts: More commonly known as "Nuns' Puffs," a French donut, lightly fried and topped with sugar.

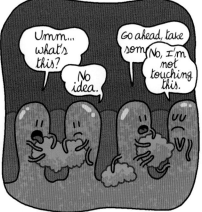

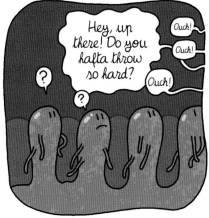

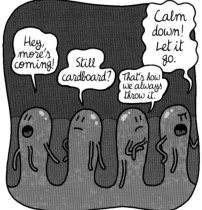

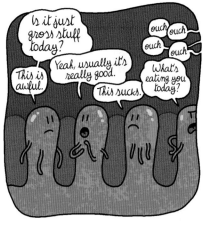

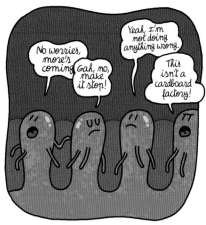

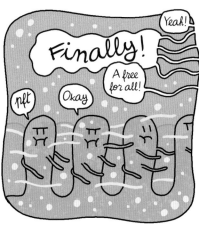

WEIRD, LITTLE-KNOWN, OR FORGOTTEN VEGETABLES...THE KIND THAT REMIND YOU OF THE GREAT DEPRESSION. AN INCOMPLETE LIST:

A WELL-KNOWN CHEF (I NO LONGER REMEMBER WHICH ONE) ONCE SAID ON THE RADIO:

WINTER VEGETABLES

YES, WELL... WE FORGOT ABOUT THESE VEGETABLES FOR A REASON! HAHA! KNOW WHAT I MEAN?

BOOHOO

FOR COOKING! (AND EATING)

WHAT'S THIS? SOME KINDA GUIDE?

HIPSTER → HEYY, CHECK OUT ALL THESE ORGANIC VEGGIES! IT'S JUST LIKE PORTLAND!

I'M GOING TO LEARN THEM ALL AND MAKE A SWEET VEGAN SOUP!

NORMAL PERSON →

PARSNIP

A **PARSNIP**, CLOSE COUSIN TO THE CARROT, CAN BE EATEN RAW, PEELED, AND GRATED; FRIED INTO CHIPS; MASHED OR STEWED. IN OTHER WORDS, WHEN DICED, IT BASICALLY COOKS LIKE A CARROT. IT TASTES SLIGHTLY SWEET AND MILDLY LIKE HAZELNUTS.

KOHLRABI

ADD TWO EYES AND A MOUTH, AND YOU'D SAY THIS WAS AN AXOLOTL (MEXICAN WALKING FISH) WITH LEAVES (THAT COOK UP LIKE SPINACH) FOR GILLS. WASH IT, PEEL IT, AND EAT IT MASHED, IN SOUP, OR SAUTÉD. IT COOKS IN FIVE TO TEN MINUTES IN BOILING WATER; DICED FINELY, IT CAN EVEN BE EATEN IN A SALAD.

CHERVIL ROOT

IT'S PRETTY RARE, BUT IT TASTES LIKE A CROSS BETWEEN A POTATO AND A CHESTNUT. AFTER BEING WASHED AND PEELED, IT'S DYNAMITE AS FRIES, MASHED, OR IN A STEW. BASICALLY, YOU CUBE IT UP, AND CHECK ITS DONENESS BY PIERCING IT WITH A FORK.

CHINESE ARTICHOKE

YOU WOULD THINK THESE ARE LITTLE EARTHWORMS IN A FARMER'S PLANTING TRAY. (THEY'RE NOT.) CHOOSE THE VERY WHITE ONES, CLEAN THEM, AND SIMMER THEM IN WATER OR BROTH FOR ABOUT TEN MINUTES. NEXT, GENTLY SAUTÉ THEM, AND YOU'LL FIND THEM TO BE SUBTLE AND TASTING LIKE ARTICHOKE OR SALSIFY.

RUTABAGA

PEEL AND COOK THEM FOR A VERY LONG TIME (AROUND AN HOUR) IN WATER. THEY'RE GREAT IN A STEW OF BEEF OR PORK, MASHED, OR EVEN IN CHIPS. THEY TASTE SIMILARLY TO A TURNIP, JUST MORE POTENT. YOU CAN EVEN GRATE IT IN A SALAD WITH SOME CARROTS.

BLACK RADISH

YOU ALREADY KNOW EVERYTHING ABOUT THIS VEGETABLE BECAUSE OF TO DRINK AND TO EAT 1. YOU EAT BLACK RADISHES EACH WINTER, AND SOME OF YOU EVEN KNOW ITS SONG BY HEART.

GOLDEN TURNIP

UNLIKE THE PINK AND WHITE TURNIP, THIS TURNIP IS NOT BITTER; INSTEAD, IT'S RATHER SWEET. GOOD NEWS: IT COOKS IN THE SAME WAY.

JERUSALEM ARTICHOKE

WITH ITS SUBTLE TASTE REMINISCENT OF ARTICHOKE HEARTS, IT'S GREAT IN CHIPS, MASHED, STEWED... YOU JUST HAVE TO SCRUB IT WELL. IT COOKS PRETTY QUICKLY (SAUTÉED IN BUTTER, FOR EXAMPLE). UNFORTUNATELY, HOW SHOULD I SAY IT...IT REALLY MAKES YOU FART.

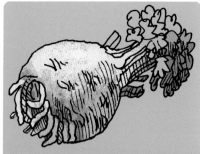

CELERY ROOT

FORGET THE "ANTS ON A LOG" YOUR GRANDMA MADE...SHREDDED IN SALAD, CELERY ROOT IS EXQUISITE. IN SOUP, MASHED, OR AS FRIES, IT'S ALSO GOOD. YOU SHOULD PEEL IT BEFORE COOKING, AND YOU CAN SAVE ITS LEAVES FOR DRYING AND ADDING AROMA TO A VARIETY OF DISHES. THE TASTE IS SPICY-SWEET.

SALSIFY

AVOID THEM CANNED; FRESH IS WAY BETTER. THEY HAVE TO BE PEELED, WHICH IS SUPER ANNOYING. BUT THEY'RE VERY GOOD WITH A CREAM SAUCE OR SAUTÉED IN BUTTER AFTER YOU'VE SIMMERED THEM FOR THIRTY MINUTES OR SO. BUT THEY'RE SUPER SHITTY TO PEEL. UP TO YOU.

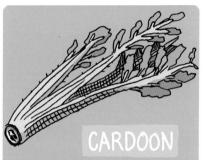

CARDOON

IT TASTES STRONGLY OF ARTICHOKE HEARTS. YOU MUST PEEL IT, SEPARATE THE STALKS, AND CUT IT INTO PIECES. NEXT, COOK IT FOR FIFTEEN AND THIRTY MINUTES IN SIMMERING WATER. IDEAL IN A GRATIN, WITH BONE MARROW, OR WITH TRUFFLES, IF YOU PAY AN ARM AND A LEG FOR SOME OR OWN A TRUFFLE-HUNTING PIG.

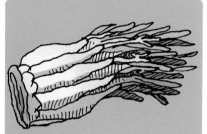

PUNTARELLE

GREENS THAT ARE EASY TO FIND IN SWITZERLAND BUT ARE RIDICULOUSLY EXPENSIVE IN PARIS. A KIND OF ITALIAN CHICORY, IT IS LESS BITTER THAN ENDIVES AND VERY CRUNCHY. ITS LEAVES COOK LIKE SPINACH, AND ITS HEART CAN BE EATEN RAW. AFTER YOU SEPARATE THE STALKS, OF COURSE.

HORSERADISH

ONLY EATEN SHREDDED AFTER HAVING BEEN PEELED AND ITS CORE REMOVED. YOU CAN USE IT TO MAKE CONDIMENTS THAT SET YOUR MOUTH ON FIRE AND DISSOLVE YOUR GUMS. THE JAPANESE USE IT FOR WASABI. WELL, NOT HORSERADISH, BUT ITS COUSIN.

PARSLEY ROOT

A MILD, SWEET, AND PARSLEY-LIKE FLAVOR. MAKE SURE TO PEEL IT FIRST. THEN, EAT IT RAW, IN A SALAD, FRIED INTO CHIPS, MASHED, STEWED, OR SAUTÉED. TO GIVE YOU AN IDEA, IT COOKS IN SIMMERING WATER FOR ROUGHLY TEN MINUTES.

OXALIS TUBEROSA

OR, PERUVIAN OCA TUBER. NO NEED TO PEEL IT; JUST SCRUB IT WELL AND COOK IT A LITTLE LESS THAN YOU WOULD POTATOES. GOOD STEAMED, SAUTÉED, OR ROASTED. ITS FLAVOR IS CHESTNUT-Y WITH A HINT OF ACIDITY. FIND A GOOD LOS CALCHAKIS ALBUM, AND GO, BABY, GO!

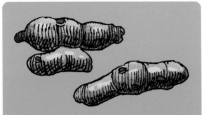

PALE-LEAVED SUNFLOWER

IT'S KIND OF LIKE JERUSALEM ARTICHOKES THAT DON'T MAKE YOU FART, OR SALSIFY THAT ISN'T A BITCH TO PEEL. PEEL IT, WASH IT, AND COOK IT VERY LITTLE BECAUSE ITS TASTE IS FRAGILE. SAUTÉED, MASHED, OR STEWED, IT'S ONE OF THE BEST "FORGOTTEN" VEGETABLES.

RED RADISH AND GREEN MEAT RADISH

ARE TWO RATHER FUNNY BI-COLORED RADISHES. THEY'RE DELICIOUS IN CARPACCIO, OR SHREDDED, OR PICKLED. YOU CAN ALSO COOK THEM, BUT IT'S LESS INTERESTING.

MASHUA TUBERS

THEY LOOK A LOT LIKE OXALIS TUBEROSA, AND THEY'RE ALSO FROM SOUTH AMERICA. WHEN RAW, THEY TICKLE THE GUMS, BUT WHEN COOKED THEIR TASTE BECOMES MILD AND SWEET. THEY HAVE THE REPUTATION OF BEING AN ANAPHRODISIAC, BUT I HAD SOME LAST NIGHT AND I...HOLD ON...WHAT'S GOING ON...

SWISS CHARD OR JUST CHARD,

DEPENDING ON WHERE YOU'RE FROM. ITS LEAVES CAN BE RINSED, COOKED LIKE SPINACH, OR EATEN RAW IN A SALAD. WHILE WIDELY AVAILABLE FOR CONSUMPTION, SWISS CHARD, LIKE SPINACH, CONTAINS OXALIC ACID, A FACTOR IN KIDNEY STONES WHEN EATEN IN LARGE QUANTITIES.

VITELOTTE POTATO

IS A PURPLE POTATO THAT COOKS LIKE A NORMAL ONE BUT TASTES LESS GOOD. BUT IT'S ALL THE RAGE AMONG FANS OF JEDI MACE WINDU AND MADAM MIM.

CARROT

YELLOW, WHITE, OR RED, IT IS PREPARED JUST LIKE THE ORANGE ONE. TO BE EATEN RAW TO APPRECIATE THE SUBTLETIES OF ITS TASTE, STEWED, OR MADE INTO A TATIN BY CHRISTINA PIRELLO. APPRECIATED BY RABBITS, CARROTS WILL ALSO CAUSE THEM TO POOP IN AN IDENTICAL COLOR...NO, JUST KIDDING.

BEET WHETHER YELLOW,

RED, CHIOGGIA, OR CRAPAUDINE, BEETS ARE DELICIOUS RAW (AFTER HAVING BEEN PEELED), IN CARPACCIO, OR ROASTED ON PARCHMENT PAPER IN THE OVEN, WHICH SWEETENS THE TASTE.

KALE

ONLY THE LEAVES ARE EATEN, EITHER RAW (MARINATED AND MASSAGED WITH OIL, SALT, AND LEMON), ROASTED INTO CHIPS IN THE OVEN, OR SAUTÉED LIKE FUCKING CABBAGE. CURRENTLY A FAVORITE OF HIPSTERS (2015).

LONG TURNIP HAS A

TASTE THAT'S LESS PRONOUNCED THAN THE PINK AND WHITE ONES. PEEL IT IF ITS SKIN IS TOO THICK. YOU CAN EAT ITS LEAVES IN SOUP OR SAUTÉED WITH SOME PORK (FOR EXAMPLE). FOR THE REST, YOU HAVE YOUR CHOICE MASHED, IN SOUP, STEWED WITH PORK, OR RAW IF THE ROOTS ARE YOUNG.

lon.

lon.

Instant ramen

TODAY WASN'T YOUR FAVORITE. EVERYTHING WENT WRONG, AND YOU DON'T FEEL LIKE COOKING.

Man, and I didn't even get groceries.

Whatever. I'll just have some ramen.

HOWEVER, IN YOUR FRIDGE, THERE'S A FEW PICKLES, SOME OLD SRIRACHA, A CAN OF TUNA, AND THE REST OF—

Really, it's okay.

I like ramen. It takes five minutes.

One packet, some water...

...then, bed.

AHH, INSTANT RAMEN...A DISH THAT'S FULL OF HISTORY. EVEN IF THE WORD MAY BE CHINESE ("STRETCHED PASTA"), THE NOODLES TOOK OFF IN JAPAN AT THE BEGINNING OF THE 20TH CENTURY.

AND SIXTY YEARS LATER, MOMOFUKU ANDO INVENTED THE CONCEPT OF INSTANT RAMEN.

THANKS TO THE TECHNIQUE OF DEHYDRATION BY HOT OIL

Sorry, but...can't I just make my ramen in peace?

What's this, the History Channel?

It just takes five minutes!

Then, bed.

FIVE MINUTES... HAVE YOU NEVER ASKED YOURSELF:

WHY INSTANT FOODS TAKE SO MUCH TIME?

There's even a recipe... What does it mean?

진라면

WELL, LET'S GO BACK TO THE END OF THE 1950s WHEN INSTANT FOOD WAS RAPIDLY GROWING IN POPULARITY...

Seems like this is coming from the drop ceiling.

This is ruining my evening.

COME ON, STOP!

AT THE BEGINNING, THE METHOD WAS STRAIGHTFORWARD. COOKING THIS KIND OF FOOD WAS BASICALLY...INSTANT.

POOF!

EXCEPT THAT THE HOME COOK WASN'T INTERESTED. IT WAS A FLOP, OR RATHER, A POOF.

So when do I stir?

When do I add pepper?

POOF

NO ONE FELT LIKE THEY WERE COOKING. COOKS DIDN'T FEEL USEFUL OR VALUED.

THE MARKETING GUYS HAD ANOTHER MEETING...

She needs more stirring.

We need more steps.

Yeah, she feels guilty with the lack of effort.

Isn't this sexist to base our product on her?

Have you ever seen a man cook?

Well, no.

See?

AND, A FEW YEARS LATER, INSTANT FOOD WENT BACK ON THE MARKET.

THIS TIME, LESS DIRECT. WITH STEPS, AND OFTEN, A "RECIPE."

Bring 2½ cups of water to a boil. Add the soup base, and—

Well, this is no Julia Child, is it.

Forget this.

...

Ahh.

I think it's finished.

I'll be able to eat in peace.

Oh, shit!

Now it's coming from below!

STOP! THAT'S ENOUGH!

QUIET!

THIS "RECIPE-BASED" MARKETING WOULD PAY OFF: IN 2012, 100 BILLION UNITS OF INSTANT NOODLES WERE SOLD WORLDWIDE. MOMOFUKU ANDO HIMSELF ATE THEM REGULARLY. HE DIED AT AGE 96 YEARS, ALMOST INSTANTANEOUSLY.

leon.

It doesn't matter... I've ALWAYS hated Swiss chard!

For as long as I can remember.

Creamed or in tomato sauce, their consistency and taste made me think of human skin soaked in bile.

That's why, when a cold winter day someone offered me some CARDOONS (that pretty much look like chard), I politely declined.

This refusal lasted for over 19 years.

I was in the wrong, because I later learned that Swiss chard is as different from a cardoon as a Roman consul is from a penguin.

CRRRRK

It's quite an image, but I give credit when it's due.

To avoid this (very common) mistake, you just have to refer to biology.

CARDOONS are an herbaceous plant from the artichoke and thistle family.

SWISS CHARD is an inedible vegetable from the cockroach family.

(The difference is subtle.)

Tasting cardoons for the first time in one's life is a true mystical experience...

Lea... m... a...

Wow, an artichoke heart!

Haa!

Gahhh!

It's really good.

Save me!

A real taste bud bait and switch.

The best way to cook this vegetable is to make a...

CARDOON GRATIN

For this, you'll need (for four people, let's say):

flour   salt   pepper

A generous 3 lb of cardoons

butter   crème fraîche

grated cheese   a lemon   oil

A friend (if possible, a farm-to-table restaurant owner)

First, the cardoons. Sorry, but you'll figure it out:

Separate the branches and remove all the leaves:

Peel the "heart" generously and cut it in four:

Peel each branch just as generously, and cut them into 1½ inch pieces. Chuck any that look gross.

yes   no

The task is extremely long and tedious (my poor mother, from whom I took this recipe, died while peeling cardoons). If you have a friend who owns a farm-to-table restaurant, this is where he comes in:

I repainted the Sistine Chapel with a Kolinsky 610.

Cardoons don't scare me!

Of course, you can get peeled, canned cardoons, but they're not as good and

I'M DONE.

No worries.

See you around. Time for my social security benefits.

② As soon as your cardoons are ready, submerge them into water with a little lemon so they don't turn black (take another look at the previous image).

Next, cook them in salted, boiling water for a good thirty minutes for small cardoons or a little longer for larger ones:

40 MINS. 30 MINS.

a big one · a small one · (the "heart," too)

③ During this time, you're going to make the sauce. If you have saucière hanging around in some corner of your kitchen, now's the time to break it in:

I'M READY!

If not, a saucepan works, too. Begin by heating a little oil or butter (or both).

TSHHHHH

Next, add a heaping spoonful of flour and let it brown while stirring over low heat. Maybe you don't realize it, but you're actually making a roux.

That's me!

("Roux" is also a French word for redhead.) Anyway. Add equal quantities of crème fraîche and water (or, even better, the water you boiled the cardoons in):

The idea is to have a generous amount of sauce for your cardoons, so you figure out the exact quantities, 'kay?

④ Okay. The cardoons are cooked* (and drained), and the sauce is more or less well-made. It's now time to mix it all together and top with grated cheese.

Season with salt and pepper and brown for 20 minutes or so at 350°F (in short).

AND IT'S READY!

*TENDER BUT NOT MUSHY

If, just before serving, you shave a little fresh truffle on top, it's to die

It's funny, this fixation on cardoons...

For me, it's turnips. I never could stand the fucking w...

WHAT?

Wait a moment, Doctor... Do you have any idea WHO I am?

N...no, but--

You lie down, and I'll restart the timer!

But--

Shsh!

So, I hear you don't like turnips, mmm?

It took me less than an hour to convince the bogus psychologist about turnips... And I even did it for free! **THIS HAS BEEN A MESSAGE** from the Association of Turnips, Celery, Spinach, Brussels Sprouts, and Other Reject Vegetables that Can Actually Be Delicious. (A.T.C.S.B.S.O.R.V.T.C.A.B.D.).

VIVE LA VICTOIRE!

I digress.

lon.

^oysters (with Foie Gras)

THIS IS THE EASIEST RECIPE OF THE THREE AND ALSO THE MOST EXPENSIVE. YOU'LL NEED:

foie gras

oysters

chives

pepper

oyster death party!

*A friend

ⓐ MAKE YOUR FRIEND SHUCK THE OYSTERS, AND USE THE TIME TO ADVANCE A LITTLE ON CANDY CRUSH™.

Shit. Can't you help me for a little?

No. I need my hands. I'm an artist.

SWEET

EMPTY THEIR WATER, WAIT A LITTLE, AND EMPTY THEM A SECOND TIME.

ⓑ CUT THE FOIE GRAS INTO ¾ X 2 INCH STRIPS:

Oh no, I did ½ by 1½.

NO WORRIES. JUST MAKE SURE YOU CUT THE CHIVES <u>EXACTLY</u> ONE MILLIMETER EACH.

↖ 1 MM

ⓒ ON AN OYSTER, LAY A STRIP OF FOIE GRAS, ADD THE CHOPPED CHIVES, AND SEASON EVERYTHING WITH PEPPER:

(REPEAT WITH THE OTHER OYSTERS.)

ⓓ PLACE UNDER THE BROILER FOR FIVE TO TEN MINUTES, OR HOWEVER LONG IT TAKES FOR THE FOIE GRAS TO BROWN A LITTLE. CREATE A DIVERSION, AND SERVE AT ROOM TEMPERATURE:

mmm!

Hey, not bad I... SWEET

TASTY

♫

* C.F. TDTE 2

② Carpaccio of Coquilles de Saint-Jacques

A LITTLE HARDER TO MAKE, BUT LESS EXPENSIVE. THIS RECIPE NEEDS (FOR FOUR):

fresh coquilles de Saint-Jacques (scallops)

balsamic vinegar

olive oil

passion fruit

radish sprouts

salt and pepper

St. Jacques, son of Zebedee

ⓐ PUT THE SCALLOPS IN THE FREEZER FOR A GOOD TEN MINUTES:

brrr

(HOWEVER MANY YOU WANT, OKAY. IT'S YOUR DISH.)

THIS WILL MAKE IT A LOT EASIER TO CUT THIN SLICES:

APPROXIMATELY 0.2 MM THICK

ⓑ WHILE THE SCALLOPS ARE FREEZING THEIR TITS OFF, MAKE THE VINAIGRETTE.

CUT THE PASSION FRUIT IN TWO.

STRAIN THE PULP WITH A TEA BALL OR A FINE MESH STRAINER:

NO NEED TO KEEP THE SEEDS!

ⓒ IN A BOWL, MIX THE PASSION FRUIT JUICE, A TABLESPOON OF VINEGAR AND 2-6 TBSPS OF OLIVE OIL:

SEASON WITH SALT AND PEPPER

FINALLY, ON A LARGE PLATE, DRIZZLE THE COQUILLES DE SAINT-JACQUES WITH THE VINAIGRETTE.

ⓓ SERVE EVERYTHING ON A PRETTY BED OF RADISH SPROUTS (IT'S CLASSY), AND YOU'RE GOOD TO GO.

(No class.)

(Class.)

ST. JACQUES'S OPINION:

With nut oil instead of the vinaigrette, it's also not bad.

It's less of a pain in the dick to make, too.

Right!

3 shrimp avocado Grapefruit

PRETTY EASY AND NOT TOO EXPENSIVE, UNLESS YOU MAKE IT WITH SMOKED SALMON INSTEAD OF THE SHRIMP. FOR FOUR SERVINGS, YOU'LL NEED:

two grapefruit

two ripe avocados

a bunch of shrimp

a lemon

olive oil

salt and pepper

paprika

---

a PEEL THE GRAPEFRUIT AND ROUGHLY CHOP ITS SEGMENTS:

(Get to knifin'!)

DO THE SAME WITH THE AVOCADOS:

(Pain in the ass!)

---

b PEEL THE SHRIMP IF YOU HAVE BOUGHT THEM UNPEELED, AND COOK THEM IF YOU BOUGHT THEM RAW (WHICH MEANS YOU'RE EITHER A REAL DUMMY OR A REAL CHEF):

JUICE THE LEMON:

I never knew how to do this! Whoa!

---

c MIX THE AVOCADO, SHRIMP, AND GRAPEFRUIT INTO CONTAINERS:

IF IT'S CHRISTMAS EVE, YOU CAN EVEN BRING OUT YOUR MASON JARS. THE IDEA IS TO HAVE SOME KIND OF CLASSY PRESENTATION. SQUEEZE SOME LEMON, AND ADD A DRIZZLE OF OLIVE OIL.

---

d SEASON WITH SALT, PEPPER, AND A LITTLE PAPRIKA, AND YOU SHOULD GET THIS:

Whatja think?

Oh yes, classy.

A Mason jar!

I haven't seen these since 1998!

lon.

APPETIZER WITH A LEEK

FEATURING LEMMY KILMISTER OF MOTÖRHEAD

ARE YOU HERE FOR A SHOW?

NO, DUDE, I'M HERE TO MAKE YOU LIKE LEEKS.

W...WHAT DO YOU MEAN? WAIT... ARE YOU FRENCH?

YOU NOTICED THEM WHEN ROUNDING AN AISLE. FOR A SPLIT SECOND, YOU COULDN'T PLACE THEM.

Insane.

Green onions on 'roids.

What are they doing to food these days?

LEEKS. YOU'VE ALWAYS HATED THEM. DRY IN CASSEROLES, LIMP IN SALADS, STICKY IN SOUP...

THE ONLY LEAK YOU TOLERATED WAS WHEN LEMMY KILMISTER'S SONGS WERE UPLOADED TO NAPSTER, BACK WHEN YOU WERE A FAN OF MOTÖRHEAD.

OVERKILL OVERKILL OVERKILL

BUT THAT WAS BACK THEN.

WELL, I MEA

WHO THE FUCK IS CALLING ME?

L...Lem... Lemmy?

Yeah, dude.

Lemmy's in the produce section?

whaaa!

YOU SEE, DUDE. LEEKS CAN BE BANGIN'. I HAVE THIS CRAZY RECIPE THAT ABSOLUTELY KILLS.

Oh...oh, really? With leeks?

WITH LEEKS.

T...that's imp

SHUT THE FUCK UP!

You speak English?

FIRST, YOU'LL HAVE TO GET:

RED PESTO

(OR GREEN PESTO*)

MOZZARELLA

AND SOME LEEKS

*YOU CAN BUY SOME OR MAKE IT AT HOME BY MIXING TOGETHER GARLIC, OLIVE OIL, AND FRESH BASIL.

NEXT, CUT THE LEEK LIKE THIS:

AND THEN IN HALF LENGTHWISE.

THEN SEPARATE THE LAYERS AND GET RIBBONS:

(IT'S GOOD IF YOUR RIBBONS ARE ABOUT ¾ INCH WIDE.)

NEXT, COOK THE LEEKS FOR TWO MINUTES IN BOILING WATER:

DRAIN AND SPREAD THEM ON A DISH TOWEL TO HELP THEM DRY FOR A FEW MINUTES:

(OR, TWO TOWELS IF YOU DON'T HAVE ENOUGH SPACE).

NEXT, SPREAD THE LEEKS WITH A THIN LAYER OF RED OR GREEN PESTO (THE RED'S PRETTIER):

CUT THE MOZZARELLA INTO SMALL CUBES:

AND IT'S ALMOST FINISHED!

ALL YOU NEED TO DO IS ROLL THE MOZZARELLA CUBES IN THE LEEKS AND YOU'LL HAVE:

LEEK SUSHI **ROLLS!**

Hey, Lemmy, I feel better about leeks already!

But the mozzarella...

WHATEVER, IF YOU DON'T LIKE **MOZZ**, REPLACE IT WITH **FETA!**

FUCKIN' BASTARD!

...Mozart's in the produce section?

Here I am. You called?

lon.

Winter | 143

Table of Recipes

Appetizers

Entrées

Desserts

Index

Bold page numbers indicate a recipe

* Pépé Roni's Good Advice

Acknowledgements

Arbois: Florian (advice)

Barcelona: Matthieu and Jean-Christophe (logistics)
  Fernando (typography)

Besançon: Christophe (marinade)

Berlin: Julia (logistics) and Majorie (drawings and colors)

Blog: The readers (advice and motivation)

Cambremer: Stéphanie et Lucile (hospitality)

Coutances: Dominique (adventures), François-Régis and Elvira (radio)

Hambourg: Claudia and Sabrina (Mr. Carlsen), Matthias (energy)

Geneva: Monique and Jean-Claude (food and advice),
  Roland (motivation)

Hyères: Fanny (advice)

Lyon: Sonia (food, advice, and motivation), Connie and Laurent (food),
  Olivier (advice), Manu (photography)

Málaga: Regina (translation)

Madrid: Catalina and Sheila (Mr. Salamandra Graphic), Jesús and
  Javier (tourisme)

Paris: Nicolas, Olivier, Muriel, and Thierry (Mr. Publisher), the team of
  leMonde.fr (maintenance), Sandrine and Pascal (hospitality and
  motivation), Ophélie (energy)

Vegas: Matthieu and Claire (colors)

On the blog, talented authors have generously shared their work:
Anne Montel and Loïc Clément, Chloé Vollmer-Lo, Daniel Blancou,
Dorothée de Monfreid, Frederik Peeters, Gally, Gilles Rochier, Guillaume
Plantevin, Greg Shaw, Hervé Bourhis, Lison Bernet, Leslie Plée, Louis-
Bertrand Devaud, Martin Vidberg, Mathias Martin, Nancy Peña,
Nicolas Wild, Obion, Philémon, Pochep, Sébastien Vassant, Terreur
Graphique, Thibaut Soulcié, Un et deux, Zelba.

Thank you.

SPICES

Later it's crushed... *It's the best!* *For enhanced flavor...* *Toast us!*

STAR ANISE (OR BADIAN) IS AN AROMATIC SEED NATIVE TO CHINA AND VIETNAM THAT IS USED TO FLAVOR EVERYTHING FROM SAVORY FOODS TO LIQUOR TO DESSERTS.

S / BS / BD

ANISE IS MOST COMMONLY USED IN PASTRIES AND MEDITERRANEAN CUISINE. IT'S ONE OF THE INDISPENSABLE FLAVORS IN GINGERBREAD.

BD

CINNAMON PERFUMES MANY SOUTH ASIAN CUISINES AND IS USED ALL OVER THE WORLD. IT'S USED IN BEVERAGES, PASTRY, AND IT ALSO GOES VERY WELL WITH WILD GAME.

BD / M / I

CARDAMOM IS AN ESSENTIAL INGREDIENT OF CURRY AND RAS-EL-HANOUT. ITS FLAVOR AND WARMTH BEING VERY PRO-NOUNCED, ONE OR TWO SEEDS CAN BE ENOUGH IN A DISH.

BS / I

CARAWAY IS A COUSIN OF CUMIN. IDEAL FOR BREADS, SAUSAGES, AND RACLETTE; IT CAN ALSO BE FOUND IN GOUDA CHEESE.

BD / FS / C

CUMIN COMMONLY SPICES MEATS, SAUCES, STEWS, AND STUFFING. IT IS USED WIDELY IN CUISINES THROUGHOUT SOUTH ASIA AND LATIN AMERICA.

M / SC / CS

TURMERIC LOOKS A BIT LIKE GINGER. RECOMMENDED BY NUTRITIONISTS, IT IS ALSO USED AS NATURAL FOOD COLORING. USED OFTEN IN MANY AFRICAN, MIDDLE EASTERN, AND ASIAN CUISINES.

BS / I

FENNEL IS MAINLY USED IN BAKING, BUT IT ALSO WORKS MARVELS ON GRILLED FISH. A KEY INGREDIENT IN MEDITERRANEAN CUISINE.

BD / FS

FENUGREEK IS VERSATILE, AS IT TASTES MUCH LIKE CELERY. IT'S USED COMMONLY IN EURASIAN AND MIDDLE EASTERN SAUCES, SOUPS, AND STEWS.

S / SC / BS

JUNIPER IS A BERRY THAT YOU CANNOT EAT, BUT IT CAN BE USED TO FLAVOR SAUERKRAUT, MARINADES, GIN, AND IT GOES WELL WITH WILD GAME.

S / M / MA

GINGER IS BEST WHEN FRESHLY GRATED, BUT IS AVAILABLE AS A POWDER. A SPICY, EARTHY ROOT THAT IS INDISPENSABLE IN BAKING, CONFECTIONERY, AND IN LOTS OF TRADITIONAL CUISINES AROUND THE WORLD.

S / BS / BD

CLOVE IS A VERSATILE AROMATIC SPICE USED IN BAKING SWEET THINGS, LIKE GINGERBREAD, AND SAVORY DISHES, LIKE POT-AU-FEU.

S / BS / MA

NUTMEG IS PERFECT FRESHLY GRATED OR PURÉED, IN A BECHAMEL OR A GRATIN. THE MACE THAT SURROUNDS IT HAS A MORE SUBTLE TASTE AND ADDS AROMA TO SAUCES AND DRINKS.

BS / SC / C

NIGELLA SEEDS (OR BLACK CUMIN) HAVE AN HERBACEOUS, MILDLY BITTER FLAVOR. IT'S COMMONLY USED IN BAKING AND IN MANY MIDDLE EASTERN AND SOUTH ASIAN CUISINES.

BD / FS

POPPY SEEDS ARE USED IN PASTRY AND IN MANY STYLES OF BREAD. THEY'RE EATEN LIKE SESAME, CAN BE PRESSED FOR OIL, AND ARE FOUND IN APÉRITIF COOKIES.

BD

CHILI PEPPERS DESERVE A PAGE ON THEIR OWN (FOR EXAMPLE, PAPRIKA IS A KIND OF CHILI). THEY ARE USED TO SPICE UP TONS OF SAVORY DISHES AND PAIR WELL WITH CHOCOLATE.

SC / BS / M

PEPPER IS SOLD IN MANY FORMS AND USED EVERY-WHERE. PEPPERCORNS ACTU-ALLY START GREEN AND WILL TURN WHITE OR BLACK (BUT NEVER PINK, THAT'S ANOTHER BERRY) AFTER DRYING.

S / SC / BS

SICHUAN PEPPER IS THE HUSK OF A BERRY FAMOUSLY KNOWN FOR ITS USE IN SICHUAN CHINESE CUISINE. IT CAUSES AN ELECTRIC, ALMOST NUMBING, SENSATION ON THE TONGUE.

S / BS

ALLSPICE IS DERIVED FROM THE WEST INDIES AND IS POPULAR FOR ITS ABILITY TO TASTE OF PEPPER, CLOVE, AND OTHER AROMATICS. MOST OFTEN SOLD AS A SPICE BLEND THAT ENCOM-PASSES THE SAME FLAVORS.

S / CS

LICORICE ROOT, EVERY CHILD'S FAVORITE. THESE CAN BE INFUSED INTO ALMOST ANYTHING AND CAN BE GROUND INTO POWDER. IT'S USED IN SWEETS AND EVEN AS AN HERBAL REMEDY.

I / SC / BD

SAFFRON IS A DELICATE SPICE WITH STRONG COLORING POWER. IT'S GENERALLY ADDED AT THE END OF COOKING, THOUGH IT IS ALSO BEING USED IN PASTRY MORE AND MORE.

S / BS / BD

SESAME, WITH ITS ROASTED TASTE, ADDS AROMA TO BOTH SAVORY AND SWEET DISHES GLOBALLY. OFTEN FOUND IN BAKING, MARINADES, AND SAUCES.

SL / BD / BS

SUMAC IS A GROUND SPICE WITH A VERY BRIGHT, LEMONY TASTE. IT'S COMMONLY USED IN MANY AFRICAN AND MEDITERRANEAN CUISINES AND BAKING.

M / BS

VANILLA IS USED TO FLAVOR PASTRIES, CANDY, AND ICE CREAM. IT'S SOLD IN PODS OR EXTRACT, THOUGH PODS ARE BEST FOR INFUSION. DID YOU KNOW IT'S ALSO VERY GOOD WITH SEAFOOD?

BD / FS

WASABI, A ROOT RELATED TO HORSERADISH, IS COMMONLY USED IN JAPANESE CUISINE. IT MAKES A SPICY AND AROMATIC ADDITION TO SALADS AND SUSHI.

FS / SL

- ● CENTRAL & SOUTH AMERICAN
- ● ASIAN CUISINE
- ● SOUTH ASIAN CUISINE
- ● MEDITERRANEAN CUISINE
- ● MIDDLE EASTERN CUISINE
- ● PRETTY MUCH EVERYWHERE

- **S** SOUP
- **CS** CHARCUTERIE AND SAUSAGE
- **C** CHEESE
- **G** GRILLING
- **I** INFUSION
- **MA** MARINADE
- **BD** BREAD & DESSERTS
- **BS** BRAISES & STEWS
- **FS** FISH & SHELLFISH
- **SL** SALAD
- **SC** SAUCE
- **M** MEAT

aromatic herbs

DILL TASTES A LOT LIKE FENNEL. USED IN BUNCHES OF STEMS AND LEAVES, IT'S USED TO FLAVOR SAUCES, FISH, LIQUOR, PICKLES, AND EVEN JAM.

BASIL IS FAMOUSLY USED IN ITALIAN AND MEDITERRANEAN SAUCES AND AT THE END OF COOKING IN TOMATO-BASED DISHES. BASIL HAS A MILDLY SWEET ANISE AROMA; PURPLE BASIL TASTES LIKE CINNAMON.

CHERVIL IS A VERY DELICATE HERB THAT RESEMBLES PARSLEY. IT'S USED FRESH WITH CRUDITÉS AND, LIKE BASIL, IS ADDED AT THE END OF COOKING TO SIMMERED DISHES.

CHIVES TASTE LIKE PURE FRESHNESS. ADD THEM CHOPPED IN A SALAD TO ADD FLAVOR TO A VINAIGRETTE, WITH FISH, AND IN FRESH CHEESES.

LEMONGRASS ISN'T RELATED TO LEMONS BUT IT IS FINELY CHOPPED AND ADDED IN TEAS, SOUPS, AND BROTHS TO INFUSE ITS FRESH GRASSY, LEMONY FLAVOR.

CILANTRO (AND ITS SEEDS, **CORIANDER**) HAS A TASTE THAT PERSONALLY DRIVES ME NUTS. IT'S USED EVERYWHERE, FROM RAW FISH TO SIMMERED VEGETABLES; FROM TACOS TO TAGINES.

TARRAGON IS THE QUINTESSENTIAL HERB FOR FISH. IT IS USED IN MANY MARINADES AND IS A KEY INGREDIENT IN BÉARNAISE SAUCE, WITH ITS NOTES OF LEMON.

BAY LEAF, TOXIC IN HIGH DOSES LIKE NUTMEG, ADDS FLAVOR TO RATATOUILLE, SOUPS, STEWS, AND BASICALLY ANYTHING THAT SIMMERS FOR A LONG TIME.

MARJORAM, WITH A TASTE SIMILAR TO OREGANO BUT SWEETER, CAN BE USED IN SIMMERED MEAT DISHES AND GOES WELL IN RABBIT. IT'S ALSO DELICIOUS WITH TOMATO-BASED SOUPS AND WITH EGGS.

LEMON BALM HAS A SWEET AND LEMONY SCENT AND IS USED TO AMPLIFY THE FLAVORS IN FISH AND POULTRY DISHES. IT'S ALSO COMMONLY INFUSED INTO DRINKS.

MINT IS FOUND IN CUISINES AROUND THE WORLD, ESPECIALLY AFRICA, ASIA, AND NORTH AMERICA. BEST FRESH, IT'S BREWED IN TEA (MINT TEA, DUH) AND TONS MORE DRINKS, ALONG WITH SAUCES AND SALADS.

MERTENSIA. I ONLY MENTION IT BECAUSE IT TASTES LIKE OYSTERS, AND I LOVE OYSTERS. GREAT TO USE WITH FISH AND IN SOUPS, FOR EXAMPLE.

OREGANO HAS A REPUTATION AS A KEY FLAVOR IN ITALIAN AND MEDITERRANEAN CUISINES. USE IT FRESH ON TOP OF PIZZA OR INFUSE IT'S FLAVOR INTO TOMATO SAUCE OR SOUP.

PARSLEY. OKAY, FINE, EVERYONE KNOWS THIS ONE. USE ITS STEMS TO FLAVOR BROTHS, SOUPS, AND STEWS. USE ITS LEAVES TO TOP ALMOST ANY KIND OF DISH. GREAT IN SALADS AND DRESSING.

ROSEMARY AND ITS FRAGRANT, ASTRINGENT TASTE IS STRONG -- GO EASY! IT'S PLENTIFUL IN MEDITERRANEAN CUISINE AND IS AMAZING WITH ROTISSERIE AND BBQ.

SARRIETTE (OR SAVORY) IS LIKE A MORE DELICATE AND LIVELY THYME. IT'S ESPECIALLY NICE WITH FRESH, SUMMER DISHES. DELICIOUS IN MARINADES AND ENHANCES ANYTHING GRILLED.

SAGE IS A WARM AROMATIC, PERFECT FOR WHITE MEATS, SEAFOOD, AND VEGETABLES. IT'S GREAT FOR INFUSING IN ANY LIQUID, FROM PASTA WATER TO LIQUOR TO TEA.

SHISO LEAF ACCOMPANIES SALADS AND VEGETABLES AND IS A KEY FLAVOR IN JAPANESE BROTHS. IT'S BEEN HAVING A BIT OF A MOMENT LATELY.

THYME IS EXCELLENT FOR FLAVORING GRILLED FOODS AND MARINADES. ADD IT TO HOT WATER WITH SOME HONEY AND LEMON TO CURE A SORE THROAT.

VERBENA ADDS A BRIGHT, MILDLY SWEET AND LEMONY FLAVOR IN BAKING, AND IS DELICIOUS IN ICE CREAM. INFUSE IT IN ANYTHING FROM ALCOHOL TO CANDLE WAX.

some spice blends

FIVE-SPICE IS A BLEND OF SPICES USED COMMONLY IN CHINESE CUISINE. IT'S A BALANCE OF SWEET, BITTER, SOUR, AND UMAMI THAT TASTES AMAZING WITH DUCK, FOR EXAMPLE.

CURRY IS A SPICE BLEND WITH A THOUSAND AND ONE USES AND PREPARATIONS. CURRY IS LOVED GLOBALLY AND AN EVERYDAY INGREDIENT IN CUISINES OF ASIA, AFRICA, AND THE WEST INDIES.

GARAM MASALA IS A STAPLE SPICE BLEND IN SOUTH ASIAN CUISINES THAT USUALLY INCLUDES CUMIN, CORIANDER, NUTMEG, AND PEPPERCORNS. IT'S ESPECIALLY EXCELLENT IN SIMMERED DISHES LIKE STEWS AND BRAISES.

RAS-EL-HANOUT IS A BLEND USED IN NORTH AFRICAN AND MIDDLE EASTERN CUISINE. LIKE CURRY, THERE ARE SO MANY WAYS TO USE IT. THE DRIVING FLAVOR OF MOROCCAN TAJINES AND OTHER DISHES IN THE REGION.

CHILI POWDER IS A MIXTURE OF TOASTED AND GROUND CHILI PEPPERS USED IN CENTRAL AND SOUTH AMERICAN CUISINES AND FAMOUS FOR BEING IN THE EPONYMOUS DISH, "CHILI."

About the Author

Guillaume Long was born in 1977 in Geneva, the land of chocolate and cheese. From an early age, he was passionate about cooking and observed his mother in the kitchen. (Though that did not mean his first attempt at bread was well-received.) Long graduated from the fine arts department of Saint-Étienne with a degree in visual communication in 2002 and won the Töpffer Prize for his comic *The Sardines Are Cooked*. Since 2009, this fine gourmet is a happy man married to humor, cooking, and comics. Long runs the gastronomic blog hosted by LeMonde.fr cleverly titled *To Drink and To Eat*.